RAMBLES ROUND MOLD

by
Charles Henry Leslie

This is a facsimile of the 1869 edition
specially produced by Cedric Chivers Ltd., Bristol
for the publisher
Cyngor Sir Y Fflint
Gwasanaeth Llyfrgell a Gwybodaeth
Flintshire County Council
Library and Information Service
County Hall, Mold CH7 6NW
2000

ISBN 1 901780 31 7

Printed in Great Britain by
Antony Rowe Ltd., Chippenham, Wilts

ST. MARY'S CHURCH, MOLD, N.E.

Rambles Round Mold

BY

CHARLES HENRY LESLIE,

TO WHICH ARE ADDED

Accounts and Descriptions of Objects

in and about the Town;

AND SUCH GENERAL INFORMATION AS WILL RENDER THE VOLUME

A COMPLETE

Guide to the Neighbourhood.

MOLD:
PRING AND PRICE, HIGH STREET.
1869

Preface.

———o———

FEW Towns have altered more in their character during the past forty years than that of MOLD.

At the commencement of that period, it was a quiet country place, only enlivened on market and fair days and at assize time, and holding little communication with the surrounding places of larger traffic; its public conveyance being confined to the carrier's waggon twice a week to Chester. Now, thanks chiefly to the convenience of a Rail Road from that city, an outlet has been made for its mineral and agricultural trade, and consequently many strangers visit the place—not all bent on trade,—but some merely as tourists; the latter enquire for guide books, or statistical accounts, and none having hitherto been compiled, this want has caused the publishers of the following pages to offer something that shall attempt to supply that deficiency. They therefore have gladly availed themselves of the opportunity afforded them of being permitted to use the remarks of a gentleman, long a resident in the town, but not a native of the place, who, seeing what a native ought to have seen first—the beauties which surrounded him,—embodied his observations in writing, and told his remarks to the public in a series of lectures; these were always listened to with interest, and many enquiries having been made whether they could be had in a printed form, it was thought they might be so arranged as to satisfy the wants of strangers, by embodying in the book such a series of statistical and descriptive details, as are always found in a guide book to a neighbourhood, without interfering with the "Rambles" themselves.

There is much that will be found noticed in the "Rambles" that ought not to be forgotten or lost sight of, and of many occurrences which have taken place, that had they happened in better known towns would have made these towns famous, such, for instance, as the battle called the "Hallelujah Victory," which, although noticed by many authors in past ages, is in the present day seldom alluded to; their accounts being scattered over many works that are only to be found in large and valuable libraries; these descriptions the present author has diligently compared, and compiled from them a relation of the victory, together with the state of society at the time, this account, he hopes, will make the event more generally known to the neighbourhood.

The other unique subjects and events noticed herein he thinks he has hardly done the justice to, their importance demands, but it is to be remembered this volume aspires only to the ephemeral title of a guide book to a small town, and it may therefore be deemed presumptuous treating at all these kind of subjects with so much notice, his answer is, they are by this means sought to be popularized, and a more able hand than his it is to be hoped will ere long do justice to the subjects he here merely brings under notice. And if thought he has been over diffuse for a ramble, still he hopes he has kept clear of the curtness of that tourist, who, travelling through Mold a century ago, sums up his admiration of the place in these lines,—

> "Pretty Mold,
> Proud people,
> Handsome Church
> Without a Steeple."

The last line authenticating the date, for at that time the Tower of Mold Church was not built.

Trusting that whoever may travel over any portion of the beautiful valley the following pages attempt to describe, they may find all the enjoyment from their "rambles" they could possibly anticipate ; and when they may hereafter refer to the descriptions herein attempted, it may bring the glad thought of the healthy feeling produced by the enjoyment of nature's beauties ; whenever these recollections are recalled,—wherever they are found,—they come to us as pleasant memorials, as kindly friends ; they enhance the pleasures of society, and they create for us, society in solitude.

C. H. L.

Mold, 1869.

RAMBLES ROUND MOLD.

IT is a remark oft repeated, and its truth generally acknowledged, that they who live in a place know the least of its history. You must not be led by this remark to suppose I purpose giving you a history of our surrounding home ; all I aspire to is merely to have a little friendly gossip concerning our locality.

The love of fatherland is but a poetical phrase for, or rather a practical phase of, what the phrenologist would call, the organ of locality finely developed. Around a place,—whether sanctified by infantine memories, or school-boy truancies, or the deeper magic of "love's young dream," or those holidays from business whereon the more mature feed sweetly, or the quiet little nook into which, after all its cares, old age subsides to snatch one hour of calm,— around a place are gathered, as to their natural centre, all our tenderest associations, or most poignant thoughts. We all ought to love—and we all do love, severally, some places more than others. Be this as it may, and wheresoever our earthly lot has fallen, let us hope that to none here such a theme as one respecting place be profitless or dull—and, albeit, it come in the seemingly untaking shape of a gossipping ramble round a town, let me venture to hope that none of my hearers will regret an hour spent here in traversing round and lingering over reminiscences of pleasant Mold.

The tendency of the age is to the universal diffusion of knowledge; and in this respect the Anglo Saxon race presents the most perfect embodiment of its spirit. France has, indeed, its literary men. Italy is still a school for the fine arts; but their claim to a high standing is due to the transcendent abilities of a gifted few. Britain's superiority, on the contrary, consists in the general spread of intelligence, which places the highest prizes of merit within the reach of energy and talent in every station of life.

If I were about to treat of some untrodden shores, or if I were meditating such a trial of your patience as a mass of a country's history involves, it would be in perfect rule and order to commence with so serious a piece of geographical intelligence as "Mold is bounded," and so forth; but seeing that we enter on this theme with home feelings as a labour of love, let us try to do away with dullness,—boundaries and figures, and archives, and statistics delight not all, nor us; they may be useful in their season, but now they are as pleasureless.

And now, as to the form which our ramble shall take. We will suppose we are a party of pedestrians—some residents of the place, the larger part strangers, the friends of the other party—we set out on some fine spring or autumn morning to have a tour of the neighbourhood, and to pick up all the news about its lions, and to remark thereon; and as, in a stranger's rambles in a place the church generally claims the first notice of wonder-seekers—and wisely too—before they look further around them, so will we, then, with our beautiful church before us, make it our starting point.

Poetry and prose have laboured from age to age to describe the pictorial beauty and the moral power of what may be termed the "church landscape" of Britain, yet no description can adequately convey an idea of its pleasantness, or of its elevating influence over a people. The first sight of the spire of his native village after years—long years of wandering—has shaken many a high and firm heart, and tears of repentance and hope, and good resolves, have been often called forth from comparatively hardened sinners by a sound of the church bell, first heard in the days of innocence and youth. There can be no loneliness, even in imagination, equal to that which the poet pictures in "Juan Fernandez"—

> "But the sound of the church-going bell
> These vallies and rocks never heard,
> Never sighed at the sound of a knell,
> Or smiled when a sabbath appeared."

In foreign countries, the richly elaborated cathedral in the great square commands our admiration; but what can we say of their meagre looking country churches, with their few trees, their rampant weeds, their neglected church-yards, their dreary interiors; with their dismal pictures and painted effigies, marking sometimes a feature in the scenery; but how rarely, as with us, being the sentiment, the centre, the crown and beauty of a whole?

Whatever may be our feelings on certain points, we cannot withhold our tribute of gratitude to the spirit that has rightly restored, and fitly adorned, so many of our parish churches—whether in the crowded city, in the village, or amid the genial solitudes of our country. Suppose we take our stand on the summit of our Baily Hill, and look forth upon the beautiful valley spread before and around us—a landscape wealthy in the gifts of tranquillity and hope, and in the varied beauty of sunshine and shade—there arises before us the tower of the village church—the church of Mold. Solemn and yet pleasing associations crowd upon us; for centuries it has been the beacon to thousands whose graves are at its base. They may not have been "Village Hampdens," but they have fulfilled the mission allotted to them by Providence, and sleep—these

"Rude forefathers of the hamlet,"

beside the homes in which they lived, and under the shadow of the church in which they prayed.

What scenes of love and life, of joy and sorrow, have alternated here—come and gone—as time ceaselessly passed onward. Generations after generations have seen the soft cheeks of youth wither into the wrinkles of age, and the step so light over moss and harebell become slow and heavy, then feeble and uncertain, tottering at last from the supporting crutch into the quiet grave. Surely are those village spires the lights of our land: come and gone! come and gone! are all around; yet, ever enduring, ever inviting, ever rewarding, they continue. Age after age passes, their peaceful bells are heard above the "crash of empires;" while fears of change alarm the world, "perplexing monarchs," they discharge their mighty yet simple task—

"Invite to heaven and point the way."

The dimensions of Mold Church, are from the east to west (exclusive of the tower, which is 22 feet) 102 feet, so the whole is 124 feet. These dimensions do not include the apse which was added to the original building in the year 1856. The breadth of the body and side aisles is 61 feet, the body being 24 feet, and each aisle 16 feet, and the pillars two feet and a half square; the height of each side aisle is 24 feet. The interior of the church is spacious and handsome, consisting of a nave with aisles from which it is divided on either side by seven arches, whose clustered columns with other appropriate architectural details are of exceeding good design.

Between the springs of every arch is an angel holding a shield, on which are carved the arms of benefactors or the instruments of the passion. Among the heraldic devices, the armorial bearings of the Stanleys, who long possessed the manor, and also held sovereign sway in the Isle of Man, are very frequent. The Tower is a comparatively modern structure having been built so late as 1768, it is about 90 feet high, and is a solid and conspicuous object in the landscape. The body of the church in its interior, in process of time, was disfigured by an unsightly gallery at its west end, and those square boxes called pews and other modern excrescences, the consequence of which was not only an obscuration and defacement of its architectural beauty, but a great loss of available space for congregational worship.

About the year 1853, when the late Dean of St. Asaph was Vicar of Mold, it was wisely resolved to restore, improve, and enlarge the church; for which purpose the efficient services of that eminent architect Mr. G. G. Scott of London, were engaged. A generous impulse was given to the good work by John Wynne Eyton, Esq., and other benefactors, and the improvements were prosecuted with most commendable energy and liberality.

The old pews and gallery of former years were pulled down and the interior entirely renovated.

We will now prepare to enter our church by the north porch, through the small vestry-room; but before going in let me say step lightly here, for at the very door, almost under its threshold lie the remains of the one great artist Wales has produced, and, until the appearance of Turner, the greatest landscape painter Britain could boast of, viz., Richard Wilson. He was the son of a Welsh clergyman, and as he showed an early propensity for damaging his father's walls by covering them with curious indications of men and animals by means of a burnt stick, this induced a relative by his mother's side—she was of the Wynne's, of Leeswood—to send the youth to London, where he was placed under the care of a portrait painter, and at painting faces he continued until he was about 36 years of age, when accident determined Wilson to study landscape painting; and for this purpose he visited Italy, and after a residence of six years in the sunny south, we find him again in England, full of hope and ambition, about the year 1753. But he found the great folks would pay for their faces, but not for the glowing landscapes he threw upon the canvas. He had the feeling of the poet when he went out into the country, and looked upon the scenes of beauty spread around him, and he came back to his studio full of creative power and hope for the future. But promise after promise faded like the leaves of autumn, and the men who followed and flattered the ruling fashions of the day forgot him while he was painting his most glorious productions, until his very existence seemed to depend upon the pawnbrokers to whose hands many of his fairest works were consigned wet from the easel. " Why, look you, Dick," said one of these worthy gentlemen, who had a number of his landscapes stowed away among dusty lumber, "you know I wish to oblige, but see! there are all the pictures I have paid you for these past three years." And these were the sunny canvases— which connoisseurs now eagerly run after offering large rolls of bank notes in exchange for them.

When talent in any particular direction has missed the mark at which it aimed, the fall is often rapid. We are too apt to leave the one who has been singled out from the crowd to the fate which awaits him. Success is the idol of our sympathy. As age came upon Wilson, he had to endure all the privations of poverty; but when sight was failing—when the skilful hand had almost forgot its cunning—and his manly spirit—manly—throughout his continual battle with fortune—was beginning to droop, there came help at last, in the announcement that, through the death of a brother, a small estate had become his. His aunt, Miss Jones, resided then at Colomendy, by Llanferres; she sent him an invitation to come and live there, and there he immediately took up his residence among the beauties of natural scenery he loved so well, and which he had done so much towards illustrating; there he passed the remainder of his days, enjoying the glorious views by which he was surrounded, and the respect of his neighbours, and there he died, in May, 1782, in the 69th year of his age.

And now we will enter the church. I have, at various times, had the great pleasure of shewing several of my friends, strangers to Mold, this our church, and invariably their first exclamations when introduced within its walls have been "how beautiful," or "magnificent," or "gloriously grand," or "how exceedingly light and elegent," indeed on every occasion I have noticed the surprise evinced that such a magnificent specimen of church architecture should be found in a quiet town in Wales; and certainly it must appear to strangers surpassingly grand—for let each of us call to mind all the parish churches we may have worshipped in during our lives, can we recollect one so surpassingly fair as this? I have heard it said by those well able to give an opinion upon such matters, that its interior is more beautiful than that of any other church in the principality; but it has other matters of interest for us, for independent of its architectural beauties, there are records of the dead to claim our attention.

I suppose there must be something intuitive in me for love of antiquities in stone, for among my earliest recollections is one of stopping at the gate of a stone-mason's yard in London, whenever I was led past it—for I could not at that time have been more than seven or eight years of age—to gaze with wonder upon a number of mutilated fragments of statues there stored, which had been removed from a part of a very old abbey that stood not far from where I was born and lived, viz., Bermondsey, which is a manor and parish of itself, doubtless from having been of old an ecclesiastical domain.

Beordmund's Eye, or Eyot, or Islet, is a name referable to times when a Dane or Saxon so named possessed here a portion of terra-firma in the midst of the surrounding swamp. Bermondsey has at present few celebrities, but once it had great glories—it had a princely Cluniac convent, which numbered in succession, sixty-eight priors and six abbots, where several of our earlier kings have held their courts, where Katherine of France somewhile lived and died, and where hundreds of crusading nobles congregated before departure. Of this nothing now remains but a few old deeds and seals to testify its once existence. And what has all this to do with Mold church? methinks I hear some one say—patience, and you shall hear! Of these abbots of Bermondsey priory, one became a Bishop of St. Asaph in 1536, and the oldest monument in Mold church is erected to the memory of this abbot—his name was Robert Wharton, alias Parfew. Pennant says he was removed to Hereford in 1554, where he died in 1557. It appears that he had been a great benefactor to the churches of Gresford, Wrexham, and Mold; he is buried at Hereford, but this monument in Mold is a grateful memorial of his benevolence to the church of Mold. After this discovery you will permit me to linger in memory a little longer on the glories of Bermondsey abbey. The East Gate, which stood in what is now called Grange Walk, was pulled down about the year 1760. The great gate-house, or principal entrance, the front of which was composed of squared flints and dark red tiles ranged alternately, was nearly entire so late as about 1810; but shortly after it was wholly demolished, and the figures and ornamental stone-work of this same gateway that were thought worthy of being stored in a stonemason's yard, were those which I used to contemplate with what I can now recognize as wonder and awe. Alas! that our fathers, fifty years ago, had no Archæological Societies! We believe and hope that no such sacrilege against old time and fine taste—not to say religion also—can ever occur again.

Next in importance I put the monument placed in the church by the Rev. Doctor Wynne during his lifetime, his reason for so doing being recorded on the marble, viz., " as he scorned flattering of others while living, he had taken care to prevent being flattered himself when dead by causing this small memorial to be set up in his lifetime."

Permit me to transcribe a few more words from this unique epitaph on the Rev. Doctor Wynne, composed by himself and placed in the church several years before his death occurred.

"In conformity to antient usage, from a proper regard to decency, and a concern for the health of his fellow creatures, he was moved to give particular directions for being buried in the adjoining churchyard and not in the church." This injunction was of course faithfully carried out and his grave was made in the churchyard outside the building. But as if to illustrate the "vanity of human wishes" when the church was altered and beautified in the year 1856 among the additions, a new chancel and apse were built at the east end, and in the ground enclosed by this erection was the Rev. Doctor Wynne's grave; so that his place of rest is now within the church just in front of the communion table.

Then there is that remarkable tablet to the memory of the great grandfather, great grandmother and great uncle of the present inheritor of Rhual; the first died June 18th, 1811; the next, June 18th, 1813; and the third—as the tablet so feelingly expresses it—"on a day so fatal to their family was killed June 18th, 1815; on the ever memorable field of Waterloo." Then we have the handsome monument to Sir Alured Clarke—a Field Marshal—the very highest military rank that can be attained, and very seldom bestowed upon any but crowned heads.

When the old fashioned furnishings of the church were swept away, new and handsome fittings of solid oak benches with poppyheads, together with a beautifully carved pulpit, with stalls for the clergy of the same material were introduced. The Lectern is a most beautiful carving of an eagle, with out-stretched wings—it was the gift of WILLIAM WALCOTT SHAND, ESQ. of Gwysaney Hall. A new chancel with an apse has been added and a new oak roof highly floriated was erected over the nave, of the same elegant character as that which covers the north aisle.

The surface of the walls is elaborately carved with quartrefoils and pannellings in the stone; the tracery work of the apse is also exceedingly beautiful and all the furniture of the church is fashioned of the best materials, after the most approved ecclesiastical patterns.

From the elegant roof of the chancel is suspended a very handsome *corona lucis*, of brass, and brass pendents of a similar character hang from the centre of the arches on each side of the nave, for the purpose of lighting the church.

The five windows of the apse are filled with stained glass, by Mr. Wailes of Newcastle-on-Tyne. The three central ones contain a complete historical series of the principal incidents in the Life, Passion, and Glorification of our Blessed Saviour; the two others are of a plainer character.

One of the windows is an obituary memorial of the late Colonel and Mrs. Philips of Rhual, by their children, another was contributed by J. Wynne Eyton, Esq., in memory of his father, the Rev. Hope Wynne Eyton, who was Vicar of Mold, for a long period; and the other three were placed there by a public subscription of £400, as a testimonial of respect from the parishioners for their Vicar, the late Dean Clough. Besides this series of windows which adorn the apse, the church is rich in stained glass—at the east end of the south aisle is a large and magnificent window, in memory of the late Dr. Hughes and his Wife—placed there by their children; another near it, to the memory of the late Henry Raikes, Esq. of Llwynegryn—this is also very elegant it illustrates in eight panels, the parable of the Talents. Next in date was erected in the north aisle near the organ, an elegant memorial window, dedicated to the memory of the late Vicar of Northop, the Rev. Robert Wynne Eyton, M.A., and during the past year, viz:—1868, a fourth memorial window has been added since the church's restoration—this is placed at the west end of the south aisle, and will thoroughly harmonise with the rest and compete with them in beauty, it is in memory of the late Mrs. Marston of this town, and is erected by Wm. B. Marston, Esq., in loving memory of Lizzie his devoted wife. The prominent figures are, Moses striking the rock, Christ's baptism, Christ blessing little children, Christ conversing with the woman of Samaria, and the visit of Nicodemus to Christ. When the restorations in 1856, took place a new western door-way and entrance was intended, but then left unfinished—it was not until 1864, that through the liberality of the family of the late Henry Raikes, Esq., its completion was effected; the roof of the passage is of oak, and beautifully carved in harmony with the roof of the nave, and the appearance of the interior of the church from this entrance is exceedingly fine—the whole of the expense of this alteration was borne by the children of the late H. Raikes, Esq.

In making this new entrance it became necessary to remove the massive font to the S.W. angle of the church, which is in fact now the baptistery, hence the appropriateness of the five subjects in the last named window, all alluding to water and baptism.

The restoration of the church cost the sum of £5000. The new chancel and the carved roof of the nave were the munificent gift of John Wynne Eyton of Leeswood, Esq., and the very Rev. the late Dean Clough, was a most open-hearted contributor—There is now convenient accommodation in the church for more than one thousand worshippers.

And now we will leave these monumental and architectural notabilia, and hie away out into the clear fresh air, for we have a long walk before us, so we will hurry along the main street, but pausing at the cross, look down towards the railway station, to remember the remarkable antiquity found near there in the year 1832. The history of its discovery is simply this :—

Before the alteration of the poor-laws, much employment had to be found for able-bodied paupers by the overseers of the parish ; the field in which this discovery was made, was, at that time, rented by one of the overseers of Mold. The commissioners of roads wanting gravel, had made a large opening in the road side, which bordered this field, and, after taking out as much as was required, left of course an unsightly hole there. This it was necessary to fill up, and, as there was in the field what the tenant termed "a big lump of ground," he employed a number of the able-bodied paupers to level it and wheel it away to fill up the said hole. This "lump," as it was termed, proved to be an ancient barrow or cairn ; and, from the sort of persons employed to destroy it, we cannot wonder at the havoc made of its contents. Large slabs of stone, and pieces of broken pottery, made them first aware there was something more than bare earth in the "lump." Then a number of beads was turned up; then their cupidity was awakened by the appearance of something shining bright, then a few bones. By this time the news of the discovery was circulating in the town, and many of the townspeople were hastening to the spot. And now something like system was being arranged, for the form of an entire skeleton could be made out, and the shining substance was pronounced to be GOLD. Alas! that so many Goths were among the crowd—persons, who ought to have known better, began to break pieces off this gold treasure trove, and pocket them, this mutilating what would otherwise have been the most important, and most valuable antiquity of the kind, any nation could boast of possessing. It proved to be a complete breastplate or gorget, in one entire piece, or sheet of pure beaten gold, beautifully embossed with various patterns, in high relief, over its whole surface—the skeleton within it, as he may have worn it in life, shewing the body had been buried as he fell in battle. The warrior must have been of gigantic proportions, for the part saved measured forty-one inches in length.

The society of antiquaries was eager to know something about it, and the possessor entrusted it to my care for a time to make a careful drawing of it, and send such an account of its discovery and description as I could. They soon saw its value, and came to terms with the possessor for its purchase. My drawing is published in the 26th vol. of the "Archæologia." The great regret of all antiquarians when they saw the gorget was, that it was so mutilated; for the principal disideratum was, to know the manner in which it was fastened at the back, and over the shoulders; and this it was that the Philistines prevented from ever being known, for their appropriations—converted into rings, or pins, or brooches—have prevented the world from acquiring that much knowledge. It is now in the British Museum, and there it was long considered so precious a relic that it was for many years not exposed to the public gaze, but could be seen only on application to one of the officials; but of late a place has been made for it where all may see it. With it was found, as I before remarked, the form of an entire skeleton, and many fragments of red pottery; and besides this, pieces of coarse woollen cloth, like serge, pieces of a metal which looked like copper, but which crumbled to very fine powder upon being touched; and in addition to all this there was gathered a great quantity of coloured beads—as many, as the tenant of the field told me, to use his own words—" would fill a panmug." The material of which these beads were made was evidently not glass; and to ascertain what might be their substance, our possessor of these invaluable records of the past, proved himself as great a Goth as any of his compeers—for, was it not a fact that I can vouch for, as he told me himself, it might be counted pure invention what I am now about to relate.

When I was making my enquiries concerning these beads, I said, they cannot be glass, for it was early for glass in such abundance in these islands. "No," he said, "I broke some to see what they were made of, and I thought they felt very soft under the hammer. I wondered if they would melt, so I filled the fireshovel full of them and put it on the fire, and they soon all melted away like *Rosum*" (rosin). I had one of these beads in my possession for some time, and I unhesitatingly pronounce, that was a piece of pure amber; and by his account of their melting away in the manner he described, all the others must have been the same—so here was a loss; but as these beads were not *gold* why, there was no care for them; but had they been preserved they would have proved now of greatly more value than their weight in gold. The date I assign to this burial must have been nearly two thousand years ago, or about the commencement of the Christian era.

I find I am lingering sadly on the way; however, we will now trudge on a bit faster, and go along the Wrexham road, not pausing until we get to the first mile-stone; and here we will rest again, for I want to have some talk about and concerning Pentrehobin.

This place has always had for me very interesting associations, or, perhaps, I have invested it with marvellous attributes. I think, if I were to set about trying to compose a romance or a story, I should lay my scene in this locality. It was a singular circumstance that first attracted my attention to Pentrehobin, and, when I relate it, you will possibly say it was a very puerile and insignificant one; but even trifles will awaken tender recollections. I have before observed I was born and lived my earlier years in London. Nearly all the houses there at that time were covered with peculiar shaped red tiles, called gutter tiles. I had been away from London about two years, when I came to reside in Mold, and during that time I had seen nothing covering houses but slate. I had not noticed this—but the first day I looked upon Pentrehobin House, a feeling of singular emotion passed over me, for as Sterne says—"I vow I never had my affections more, tenderly awakened; nor do I remember an incident of my life, where the dissipated spirits, to which my reason had been a bubble, were so suddenly called home." For a portion of the house was, and still is, covered with these same kind of tiles I had seen so much of in my youthful days and the sight of them brought back so many fond recollections of home and its associations, in a spot where I then was, by myself, a stranger, away, hundreds of miles from all that was dear to me, brought melancholy, although pleasurable recollections; and to this day I never pass that house but I turn my head to look upon those tiles, and always with affection.*

But to go on with our ramble, and the first object we must notice before we pass the house of Pentrehobin is a rather large mound in the field on our left, which I feel persuaded can be none other than a barrow or cairn —similar to the one denominated the "big lump of ground"—which nearly forty years ago, produced such invaluable discoveries. I have never heard of this elevation having been noticed by any one, and have seen no one in my enquiries about it that can tell me if it was ever dug into, or even ploughed over; but

---

*All pulled down and entirely removed from the house in the summer of 1862—Alas!

superstition sometimes lends information to truth, and in the case of the former cairn being opened many stories were told and believed, of persons many years before having seen sights and heard noises about the place where it was situated. One woman, in particular, was very circumstantial in her tale of having had to come from Pentre to Mold in the dead of night, and having been met by a figure on the road, dressed, as she described, "all in bright shining gold," which she could not pass, but was forced to return to Pentre.

Now, as I before said, superstition may have been floating in the air for centuries of a great chief being interred in that spot, the traditional truth being lost. From this I argue that the mound I am now noticing may be a cairn, for I have got a tangible legend respecting its neighbourhood, which I will beg to relate as it was told to me nearly forty years since, by a person in Mold who knew the neighbourhood well. Sweden has a similar legend; it is also to be found among the legends of France, and one very like it is popular in German literature, entitled "Old and New," and in the new World, also, Washington Irving's tale of "Rip van Winkle," is a burlesque relation of the same subject.‡

‡ For the outlines of the following legend, I am indebted to the late Edward Edwards, Esq., of Maesgarmon, who, as far back as the year 1830, related it to me. He was on very friendly terms with the late Thomas Mather, Esq., of Pentrehobyn, who, having been several years before engaged professionally in searching for certain documents for Sir Watkin Williams Wynn, in the library of Wynnstay, there discovered many records and parchments, once belonging to the monks of Basingwerk Abbey, and amongst them a very circumstantial account of this legend. These records came into the possession of the Wynnstay family at the suppression of monasteries, for much of the property of Basingwerk Abbey was bestowed upon this family.—C. H. L.

It is well known that when the Christian religion became established in Britain, Wales was not behind in adopting and encouraging it, and the remains of the numerous abbeys and monasteries erected and established in Wales, sufficently testify they were as zealous in this respect as their neighbours. Huge buildings they were, with a quiet peaceable aspect, surmounted by towers rising in the midst of forests. Those grey walls covered many a fault and many an error, but they sheltered men, also, who were insensible to worldly joys.

At Basingwerk, in particular, there was one who had rendered himself famous throughout the surrounding country by his piety and learning; he was a simple and unaffected man, like all men whose knowledge is great, for science is like the sea—the farther we advance the wider grows the horizon, and the less do we seem ourselves. Brother Meyrick had had, nevertheless, his season of doubt and misgiving; but after having wrinkled his brow and whitened his hair in vain disquisitions, he had at last been compelled to fall back upon the faith of little children, and then confiding his life to prayer, as to an anchor of mercy, he suffered himself to rock gently in the tide of pure love, and holy visions, and heavenly hopes.

But in a little while rough squalls began again to shake the saintly bark. The temptations of the understanding returned, and reason began haughtily to question faith. Then Brother Meyrick grew sad—

dark clouds began to float over his spirit, his heart grew cold, and he could no longer pray. Wandering through the country, he sat upon the mossy stones, lingered by the foam of waterfalls, and sauntered amidst the murmurs of the forest; but it was in vain that he sought light from nature. To all his enquiries the mountains, the leaves, and the streams, gave but one answer—the Deity! Brother Meyrick came out victorious from many of these struggles, and each time his faith was made firmer than ever, for temptation is the gymnasium of the conscience—if it does not destroy it, it strengthens it.

But after a time inquietude again came over his spirit, more keenly than ever. He had remarked that every thing beautiful loses its charm by long use,— that the eye soon grows tired of the most beautiful landscape, the ear of the sweetest music, the heart of the fondest love, and then he asked, how shall we find, even in heaven, a source of eternal joy? In the midst of magnificence and delight which have no end, will not unchangeable pleasure at last bring on ennui? What man would wish his sweetest pleasure to last for ever—no more past, and no more future, no more remembrances, and no more hopes! Thus spake Brother Meyrick, and every day his doubts became greater.

One morning he issued from the abbey before the other monks had risen, and descended into the valley. The fields still moist with last night's rain, were glistening under the first rays of the rising sun, and Meyrick strolled gently through the shady thickets on the hill-side; the birds which had but just woke from their slumbers, were perched in the hawthorns, shaking down rosy blossoms on his bald head, and some butterflies, still half asleep, flew lightly in the sun to dry their wings.

Meyrick stopped to gaze on the scene before him. He remembered how beautiful it had seemed when first he saw it, and with what transport he had looked forward to ending his days in that delightful retreat; for him, poor child of the city, accustomed to see nought but dark courts and sombre walls, these flowers, and trees, and clear air were bewitching novelties,—how quickly passed the year of his noviciate! those long rambles in the valleys, and those charming discoveries!—streams, murmuring through the corn-flags, glades haunted by song-birds, elgantine roses, wild strawberries—what joy to 'light upon them for the first time! to meet with springs from which he had not yet drunk, and mossy banks upon which he had never yet reclined! But alas, these pleasures themselves do not last long; very soon you have traversed all the paths of the forest, you have heard the songs of all the birds, you have plucked nosegays of all the flowers, and then adieu to the beauties of the country! Familiarity descends like a veil between you and creation, and makes you blind and deaf; and thus it was now with Brother Meyrick, for thus reflecting, the monk walked on, his eyes fixed on the ground, but seeing nothing, and his arms folded on his breast, he descended into the valley, crossed the stream, passed through the woods and over the hills, the tower of the convent was lost in the distance, and at length he stopped; he was on the verge of a vast forest, which extended as far as the eye could reach, like an ocean of verdure. A thousand melodious sounds met his ears from every side, and an odorous breeze sighed through the leaves. After casting an astonished look upon the soft obscurity which reigned in the wood, Meyrick entered with hesitation, as if he feared he were treading on forbidden ground. As he advanced, the forest became larger, he found trees covered with blossoms which exhaled an unknown perfume; it had nothing enervating in it like those of earth, but was, as it were a sort of moral emanation which embalmed the soul, it was strengthening and delicious at the same time, like the sight of a good action. At length he perceived farther on a glade, radiant with a marvellous light; he sat down to enjoy the prospect, and then suddenly the song of a bird overhead fell upon his ear—sounds so sweet as to defy description—gentler than the fall of oars upon a lake in summer, than the murmur of the breeze among weeping willows, or the sigh of a sleeping infant. All the music of the air and earth and water, the melody of the human voice or of instruments, seemed centred in that song.

It was hardly a song, but floods of melody; it was not language, and yet the voice spoke. Science, wisdom, and poetry—all were in it, and in hearing it one acquired all knowledge. Meyrick listened for a long time, and with increasing pleasure. at last the light which illumined the forest began to fade; a low murmur was heard amongst the trees, and the bird was silent. Meyrick remained for a while motionless, as if he were awaking from an enchanted sleep. He at first looked around in a sort of stupor, and then arose; he found his feet benumbed, his limbs had lost their agility; it was with difficulty he directed his steps towards the abbey. But the farther he went the greater was his surprise; the face of the whole country seemed changed; where he had before seen sprouting shrubs, he now saw wide-spreading oaks—he looked for the little wooden bridge by which he was accustomed to cross the river—it was gone and in its place was a solid arch of stone. On passing a hedge where some women were spreading clothes to dry, they paused to look at him, and said amonst themselves, "There is an old man dressed like the monks of Basingwerk—we know all the brothers, but we have never seen him before." "These women are simpletons"—said Meyrick, and passed on. But at last he began to feel uneasy; he quickened his footsteps as he climbed the narrow pathway which led up the hill side towards the convent; but the gates were no longer in the old place, and the monastery was changed in its appearance—it was greater in extent, and the buildings were more numerous. An ash tree which he had himself planted near the chapel, a few months before his wandering, now covered the sacred building with its foliage. Overpowered with astonishment, the monk approached the new entrance, and rang gently; but it was not the same silver-toned bell, the sound of which he knew so well;—a young brother opened the door.

"What has happened?" asked Meyrick, "is Morgan no longer the porter of the convent?"

"I don't know such a person," was the reply.

Meyrick rubbed his eyes in astonishment. "Am I then mad!" he exclaimed. "Is not this the monastery of Basingwerk, which I left yesterday morning?"

The young monk looked at him. "I have been porter here for five years," was the rejoinder, "and I do not remember to have ever seen you."

A number of monks were walking up and down the cloisters; Meyrick ran towards them and called them, but none answered; he went closer, but not one could he recognize.

"Has there been a miracle here," he cried. "In the name of heaven, my brothers, have none of you ever seen me before?—does no one know Brother Meyrick?"

All looked at him with astonishment.

"Meyrick," at last said the oldest, "there was

formerly a monk of that name at the convent, I used to hear the old men, long ago, when I was young, talking of him; he was a learned man, but a dreamer, and fond of solitude. One day he descended into the valley, and was lost sight of behind the wood. They expected him back, but he never returned; and none ever heard what became of him. But it is now a hundred years or more since then."

At these words Meyrick uttered a loud cry, for he understood it all, and falling on his knees, he lifted up his hands and exclaimed with fervor—" God it has been thy will to show me my folly in comparing the joys of earth with those of heaven; a century has rolled over my head as a single day, while listening to the bird which sings in thy paradise. I now understand eternal happiness—Lord be gracious unto me, and pardon thine unworthy servant."

Then Brother Meyrick related to the assembled monks, what had befallen him since he left the convent, and the road he had traversed, and before sun-down he peacefully expired.

A miracle so wonderful inspired the brothers to traverse the same ground; they easily recognised the landmarks he had mentioned, and the glade in which he so wonderfully rested was found to be the spot where Pentrehobyn house now stands, and the field where we are now stopping has, ever since then, and up to the present moment, preserved the memory of this legend in its name, having always been known by the title of " The Call-bird Field."

We will now proceed a short distance farther along the high road, then turn off to the right, lingering a few minutes to look at the magnificent wrought-iron gates fronting Leeswood Hall : then make the best of our way towards Nerquis, pausing by the way to look upon the unique specimen of what can only now be seen on the confines of England and Scotland—a true border house, viz., " Tower." I shall not enter here into the history of the exploits of Reinallt ap Gryffydd ap Blyddyn's hanging the mayor of Chester there in 1465, as it is a story well known in the principality; but I am rather inclined to waver in my faith as to the staple in the great hall, there shown, as being the veritable hook he was hanged to, seeing that the history of that event says, he was besieged afterwards in his tower by a force of 200 men, sent from Chester Castle to avenge the affront, but found means to escape to the neighbouring wood and permitted his enemies to enter the building, then, with his followers, rushing from his hiding-place, fastened the door and set fire to the house, roasting them alive without mercy; the woodwork and staple in the great hall, escaping from this baking seems problematical.

After traversing the high road for a short distance, we will turn our faces towards Mold, for we have hitherto had our backs to it, and begin to ascend, for now really commences our enjoyment of the exquisite landscapes the vale of Mold offers for our contemplation.

> " Now, e'en now our joys run high,
> As on the mountain turf we lie ;
> While the wanton Zephyr sings,
> And in the vale perfumes his wings ;
> While the waters murmur deep ;
> While the shepherd charms his sheep ;
> While the birds unbounded fly,
> And with music fill the sky,
> Now, e'en now, our joys run high."

So sang a true lover of nature—let us try to realize some of his enjoyment. We shall now get a bird's-eye view of our ample theme, and shall see, at a glance, how diversified and deep are its present interests, and remember in a moment how full of curious lore are its past memories.

To the eastern extremity of our view stands the ruin of Caergwrle Castle, long a British post, and converted to a castle of defence by the Romans, after their conquest of this part of Britain. We cannot enter into a sketch of all its mutations of fortune, but will notice that Edward First in June, 1282, acquired it by surrender, and bestowed it on his consort Eleanor, who made it a resting place in her journey to Caernarvon, whither she was proceeding to give the Welsh a prince and ruler born among them. Then trace we the valley thence northward, and picture the time when this portion of the vale was "so covered with woods, that Edward, before his complete conquest of Wales, was obliged to cut a passage for his army to pass through them, in the tract between Mold and a place then called Swerdewood; and to direct that nothing should be required for the damage done to the owners. I find he called in a number of cutters for this purpose; and that in the next year, not fewer than two hundred cutters and colliers (carbonarii) were summoned out of the forest of Dean, and the county of Hereford, under the conduct of Gilbert de Clare, Earl of Gloster."—(Pennant's Tour.)

Where are finer panoramas to be found than those presented from the summits of these "heaven-kissing hills," whereon we are now wandering?—match us where you can, not even excepting its neighbouring rival, the famed Vale of Clwyd—more beautiful prospects or home-telling associations than can be enjoyed from these heights.

From the earliest period of written history, Flintshire has to boast of as many points of history as any other county in Wales; standing as it does on the confines of that part of England, which our earlier monarchs so frequently visited, viz., Chester. It became the pass or entrance ground to Wales, and every part of it can show the remains of British and Roman struggles. Offa's Dyke, traversed it from Bryn Yorkin mountain to Trydden chapel, where it terminated in a very abrupt manner. A Roman road points from Caergwrle towards Mold through the fields south of Plas Teg, and another towards Hawarden; and from these marks, both of early British and Roman encampments, there seems to be ample proof that our ancestors did not then, as in the present day, shrink from the patriotic duty of self-defence; and from historic commentaries we know that, once conquered, they learned the timely wisdom of submission to their civilizing victors.

It is little in the nature of true knowledge to be curious about the trifles of barbaric occupations, so pass we to the border land-marks of our county's history; for, as we are now placed, we can, from this height,—viz., the road going through the mine works of Brynhyfryd, or appropriately termed "Mount Pleasant"—take in, in our view, nearly the whole of the county; and beyond it the hills of Cheshire, and the more remote range of those of Shropshire, Staffordshire, Derbyshire, Yorkshire, Lancashire, Westmoreland, and Cumberland.

I have challenged comparison of this our vale of Mold with the Vale of Clwyd—that is certainly of greater extent than this—but its deficiency of water is a great draw-back, and when seen from the heights surrounding it, seems flat and tame. Neither of these charges can be brought against our vale; for look any way, there is no tameness, but variety in all shapes, including the lofty mountain, the peaceful meadows, a beautiful river running through it; and beyond that, bounding the whole length of the county on its northern side, the mighty estuary of the Dee; and what interesting historical associations are centered around that Castle at Flint, where Richard II was taken prisoner in the month of September, 1399, by his cousin and rival, and afterwards sovereign of England in his stead—Henry of Bolingbroke, Duke of Lancaster—and by him led into captivity, mounted in derision, on the worst horse they could procure, along the coast of Flintshire, until safely lodged in Chester Castle, no one appearing to pity his fate; and, if we believe Froissart, his very dog left his side to fawn on his destroyer. But all this is history, and we are here to enjoy the prospect.—

> "Now we gain the mountain's brow:
> What a landscape lies below!
> No clouds, no vapours intervene
> But the gay, the open scene,
> Does the face of nature show,
> In all the hues of heaven's bow;
> Below us, trees unnumbered rise,
> Beautiful in various dyes:
> The gloomy pine, the poplar blue,
> The yellow beech, the sable yew,
> The slender fir, that taper grows,
> The sturdy oak with broad-spread boughs.
> Old castles on the cliffs arise,
> Proudly towering to the skies;
> Yet time has seen that lifts the low,
> And level lays the lofty brow,
> Has seen this broken pile complete,
> Big with the vanity of state;
> But transient is the smile of fate;
> A little rule, a little sway
> A sunbeam in a winter's day,
> Is all the proud and mighty have
> Between the cradle and the grave."

And now we will move gently onwards, often casting our eyes back to bestow a lingering look upon the beauties which an enthusiast in nature's views, never tires contemplating, until we find ourselves on the road from Mold to Ruthin, near the second mile-stone, which we pass, not stopping until we come to the remarkable stone called "Carreg Carn March Arthur," which, to a stranger, is rather a perplexing memorial; for we naturally look upon the slab, embedded in the built-up part, for an explanation of the monument, and are puzzled to put together a few of the letters that are not obliterated; but even if found they would prove of no worth in explanation of what we expect; it being in fact a record of the judgment of a very expensive law-suit. It seems that this part of the country was once debateable land, being claimed on the one part by Lord Grosvenor as part of his mineral grant of the hundred of Yale, and on the other part by the Lords of the Manor of Mold; and to decide this right, the parties had recourse to the Court of Exchequer, and a pretty expensive suit it proved to both. However, it was given in the favor of the Lords of Mold, and the boundries then defined; and Arthur's Stone, being a mark well known and not easily to be removed, it was adjudged this should be the boundary of the two counties and two parishes—Mold, in Flintshire, and Llanferres, in Denbighshire, this decision being given in 1763, and this is what this stone is set up to record. Still this is no description of "Carreg Carn March Arthur," or "Arthur's Stone," so let me relate the legend which is attached to it.

When Arthur reigned in Britain, like all monarchs, he had his enemies to contend with, and the tale runs that—one day, being hard pressed, and retreating over these hills, his life was saved by the fleetness of his steed, which coming to an abrupt precipice, had to jump for his life; it was from one of these surrounding hills he leaped, and alighted on this spot with such force, that his two fore feet left their impressions on the solid rock some inches in depth.— Now a mark in the rock certainly appears as if made by two hoofs of a horse, and when I first saw the rock—that is about forty years since—it was considerably above the level of the road that passes by it, but in the course of these years, the accumulation of materials for repairs, has raised the road as much above the stone; and perhaps in process of time, and when the ill-built wall above it falls to ruin, it may become buried and altogether forgotten; but if any one will be at the trouble of clearing away the *debris* that has accumulated on the spot under the small arch that is built immediately over the stone, they may satisfy themselves, that there is an indentation in the rock of the exact form that would be made by a horse setting his two fore feet on soft mud, or clay, and the accidental mark on this stone taking this form no doubt gave rise to the legend.

But my chief reason for wandering thus far is, that we may turn up the bye road at the back of this stone, and make our way to the top of the rocks, facing the "Loggerheads," for here, those who have never been this way, will be gratefully surprised by the view from this height, of one of the prettiest vallies in any part of our beautiful neighbourhood; and those who have before seen it will not tire at looking on it again! for who has not felt the truth that "A thing of beauty is a joy for ever!" And here we get a full view over the spot Wilson ended his days in; and it must be a cold soul indeed who could look on such scenes as are here displayed, and not feel some of the inspiration he fed upon.. I have often stood upon these rocks, and in contemplation brought some of Wilson's paintings before me, and thought I could recognise in the view presented from these heights, his large grand masses of middle ground rock—his blue water, coming against a warm foreground—his skeleton tree branches, and his diagonal bit of fallen tree. This mannerism of materials, doubtless, arose from his mode of studying nature. We have no record of his habits as a nature student, and in the absence of existing proof, or even hearsay evidence, surmise that his studies consisted of mere outlines, filled in by an effort of memory, and the outpouring of a poetic and vivid imagination. Wilson was certainly the most poetic of all our landscape painters. Three quarters of a century have elapsed since the man passed away, yet the hand of time and the merits of succeeding artists have not robbed him of one jot of fame. And when we look from this height, and picture him moving about at last in these grounds of Colomendy, and remember the neglect he had to endure in the latter part of his town life, does it not look like a stroke of retributive justice, and read more like the concluding chapter of a novel than a scene in a real life-drama—thus becoming the unexpected heir of a small estate, amongst the very scenes he had, in imagination, for the best years of his life lived upon, and there to end his days in peace and respect.

But to look about us—see the varied views presented here whichever way we turn—beauty piled upon beauty; did ever hand of painter present a more lovely scene? I must borrow again from the poet I before laid under contribution, to picture such a view as this, for my powers of description fail me.—

"And see the river how it runs,
Through woods and meads, in shade and sun;
Sometimes swift, sometimes slow,
Wave succeeding wave, they go
A various journey to the deep,
Like human life to endless sleep!
Thus is nature's vesture wrought,
To instruct our wandering thought:
Thus she dresses green and gay,
To disperse our cares away.
Ever charming, ever new,
When will the landscape tire the view;
The fountain's fall, the river's flow,
The woody vallies, warm and low;
The windy summit, wild and high,
Roughly rushing on the sky;

> The pleasant seat, the ruin'd tower,
> The naked rock, the shady bower;
> The town and village, dome and farm,
> Each give each, a double charm,
> As pearls upon an Æthiop's arm."

In the conception of this lecture it was intended to move in a circle, of which we have now passed over about one half; but the material to talk about was so abundant, and the theme so interesting that it was found impossible to crowd all the subject matter into a space occupying the customary time of detaining an audience. Therefore, as we are supposed now to be located in a most beautiful situation, and as an exploring party must pause sometimes in their peregrinations, there seems no better spot than the present to rest here, and refresh for the continuance of our journey. Looking, then, through the mind, on the beauties Nature provides for her worshippers, I will conclude this portion of our "Ramble" with the oft quoted, but not too often, lines of Wordsworth—

> "Nature never did betray
> The heart that loved her. 'Tis her privilege
> Through all the years of this our life to lead
> From joy to joy. For, she can so inform
> The mind that is within us; so impress
> With quietness and beauty; and so feed
> With lofty thoughts, that neither evil tongues,
> Rash judgments, nor the sneers of selfish men,
> Nor greetings where no kindness is, nor all
> The dreary intercourse of common life,
> Shall e'er prevail against us, or disturb
> Our cheerful faith—that all which we behold
> Is full of blessings."

It was a wild, though so romantic a spot where I left our party at the conclusion of the first portion of this lecture, and in the original conception of its composition, I had no idea of extending it to so great a length; but the subject was so very fascinating, and the materials so abundant, that, notwithstanding all I may yet have to say, no doubt many will complain that more places and events might have been noticed. But as I said in starting, "all I aspired to was to have a gossipping ramble;" therefore let no one blame me for omitting notices of things which are well known. My purpose, as I trust you will have perceived, has been to talk about objects that, in the common course of conversation, are those least canvassed. Well! we are here supposed to be on the top of the height facing the Loggerheads. Let us descend from this height along the footpath formed in so dangerous a manner down the front of this precipice; we then pause before it, and look up at the grand face of this almost perpendicular limestone rock, and ponder awhile to think of the vast upheaval of nature which produced this rent in the earth's crust, and then prepare for the wondrous impressions our senses receive the more the study of the earth's mutations reveal to us.

While natural history has been studied until the subject appears exhausted, the wonderful discoveries of an allied science, Geology, have not yet been much investigated. This arises from the circumstance that the study of organic remains is itself a science of a very recent date. Paleontology is a science but of yesterday, yet it has achieved important things. The study of the forms of animal life which existed in the earth previous to the creation of the present races which inhabit it, is replete with the highest interest.

As astronomy penetrates the mysteries of space, so geology pierces the arcana of time. The rock formations tell of the earth's mutations; and the remains which they hold, as histories of former ages, shew that the beings which possessed the earth as a dwelling-place, were as perfectly adapted to their conditions of existence, as any living examples of creative intelligence can be. It will be found that, stored in the rocks, are creations which lived and breathed ere yet the dry land was separated from the waters, and others more recent, the inhabitants of inland seas, and the immense savanahs of an early world, which, for delicacy of structure and elegance of design, are not to be surpassed by any of the productions of organic life now existing.

Whether the hydras of superstition, or the griffins and dragons which are preserved in heraldic bearings are dim outshadowings of those ancient days, preserved like a myth amongst men, it were vain to speculate, although the speculation is fraught with interest. It is, however, curious, that we find those strange remains of the old world linked to superstitions which have their origin since the introduction of Christianity.

It is evident, therefore, that those remarkable fossil forms must have excited the wonder of man ere yet science had bent to the task of studying them. The graceful form of the Nautilus, which now enjoys existence in our tropical seas, is familiar to all. A large variety of molluscous animals of the same genera have existed through all time, and their remains found in the fossil state prove them to have been amongst the earliest inhabitants of the ancient ocean. In nearly all the rocks of a lime-stone character, the remains of the Ammonites, the ancient Nautilus, have been found. In the oolite, the lias, and the chalk, varieties of these elegant shells are constantly discovered, and nearly three hundred species have been named. This notice of one genera of fossil shells, shews how wide a field for study it presents. There is another equally interesting in the fossil vegetable world.

The beauty of vegetable form has through all time won admiration. The lotus and the acanthus are rendered classical by their numerous adaptations to ornamental uses. The ivy and the laurel, the nepenthe and the convolvolus, with numerous other plants and flowers are to be found moulded and painted on works of ornament and utensils for domestic use through all ages. Numerous and ever graceful as are the forms of the living vegetable world there is a vast field within which diligent search will discover a great variety of plants which are no less beautiful, and far less common, than their living analogues—in the by-gone flora perserved so strangely in those strata which mark the mutations of our mysterious world. The flora of the carboniferous period was of a most extraordinary character—luxuriant to an extent far exceeding even that which is now exhibited in the forests of equatorial climes. Growing most rapidly and of a lax tissue, these plants were of short duration, and were, after death, rapidly converted into a mass of uniform structure, such as we have now exhibited in every bed of fossil fuel. Three hundred species of plants belong to the coal formation of Great Britain alone; and it is found that local causes with which we are not acquainted have modified in a strange manner the plastic vegetation of this period; and in what appears to be analagous positions, we find whole genera, and even orders of plants, of very opposite botanical characters, presenting a greater disparity of vegetation than countries the most remote in geographical position.

I aim at nothing more than suggesting that the fossil shells and fossil flora furnish interesting themes for study, so will I pass hastily to a brief and merely suggestive notice of the immense variety of fossil forms allied to those of the coral formations now progressing in the Pacific ocean. The largest of these, and perhaps the grandest barrier reef existing is a coral formation off the north-east coast of the continent of Australia.

Rising at once from an unfathomable ocean, it extends one thousand miles along the coast, with a breadth at top varying from two hundred yards to a mile, and at an average distance of from twenty to thirty miles from the shore, in some places increasing to sixty and even seventy miles. The great arm of the sea included between it and the land is nowhere less then ten—occasionally sixty—fathoms deep, and is safely navigable throughout its whole length, with a few transverse openings by which ships can enter. The reef is nearly twelve hundred miles long, because it stretches almost across Torres' Straits. The modern coral present to us a great diversity of structure, but they are excelled in all respects by those of the old world. The remains of these labours of insect life are exceedingly numerous; entire mountains are built for the most part with them, and the coral animal appears to have been as busy in the ocean which washed the cliffs of the Silurian boundary, as they are at the present time on the reefs of Torres' Straits and over the Indian seas.

To give an example near home to shew the extent to which these coralline formations have gone on, will be indicated by the fact that the coralline crag at Oxford is exposed at the surface, and the bottom of it has not been reached at the depth of fifty feet. One of the lime-stone beds of the middle oolite series of England, is a continuous bed of pertrified corals, retaining the position in which they grew at the bottom of the sea; and beside this, we find scattered through our oolite formations, an immense quantity of coral remains.

A most interesting specimen of this kind of rock can be made familiar to all here, as it is a portion of a noble monument in our own church-yard. Most of you must be familiar with this memorial, built over the mausoleum that contains the remains of so many members of the Rhual family; it stands on the right hand of the path after we enter the church-yard on the south side. If you will observe, as opportunity may occur, the upper block of stone which forms the pyramid of this monument, you will see that it is one entire mass of corals and shells, most of them appearing as bones, like the leg and wing bone of large birds, smoothed down to the surface. These are, in reality, animals allied to the great family of fossil Madrepora. Indeed, if we examine the stones of which some of our admired churches are built, as at Oxford and Cambridge, we shall find that the firmly integrated mass is indeed little else than shells and corals. Thus the labours of hosts of insect architects, working in the ocean which overflowed this island myriads of ages since, are now employed to form those temples which religion consecrates to the Creator of all things.

Distributed through every phase of being, the creations of Nature present a chain, each link of which is symmetrical in form and beautiful in its arrangement.

If we commence our examination with these forms of the lowest organization which appear to mark the dawn of vitality on this planet, and trace series after series through the distinguishing strata—each one marking a new epoch in the order of animal existance, and exhibiting new and constantly varied forms, we shall find that order and elegance mark the whole. Many of those strange creations, the Trilobites—and, indeed, those monsters of that ocean which appears to have prevailed over the dry land—the Saurians, do not appear upon the first inspection to bear out this assertion; but an examination of their wonderful armour will at once shew that nature, in her works, never neglects to add to their adornment, after she has provided for the necessities of each condition.

The influence of the study of Nature, in refining and purifying the human mind, has been often insisted on, and its truth is evident. No effort of human thought, which is of a merely terrestrial character, can ever rise to the truly beautiful. Whether the artist desires to paint upon his canvas, to chisel out of marble, to mould in clay, or to cast in metal, forms which shall possess the charm—the secret of inspiring a feeling of the beautiful, he must go to Nature for his inspiration. Looking into the mirror of her works, like the influence of gazing into loving eyes, he draws from it a pure, a holy inspiration, which he may—if his practised hand be obedient to his creative mind—transfer to the gross element which is to express to mankind the power of the True.

In pursuance of the route I sketched out when the previous portion of this lecture was first read, we will now proceed to follow the windings of the River Alun, which, for the singular phenomenon remarkable in its progress we are now tracing, renders it an object of note. I refer to the route its waters here take, running contrary to general river courses, viz., underground.

Two rivers only in the civilized world beside this are noted for this wonderful peculiarity. The first and most important is the Guadiana, in Spain; and to the readers of Don Quixote it will readily occur his celebrated adventure in the cave of Montesinos, for an explanation of the wonderful legends attendant upon its history; but to descend to humbler truthful prose, it originates near 39° N. lat., in a series of small lakes called Lagunas de Ruydera, and, after having run a few miles it disappears under ground, and it continues to run under ground for more than twelve miles. It issues from the earth as a strong stream between Villarta and Daymiel. The place where the river re-appears is called Los Ojos de Guadiana, (the eyes of the Guadiana). Next in importance is the River Mole, a feeder of the River Thames, which forms its junction with the last named river, nearly opposite Hampton Court. This tributary is itself produced by the union of a numerous series of small streams and brooks, some of which rise in Sussex and others in Surrey, assumes the importance of a river near Reigate, in the latter county. Winding amidst the lovely scenery of central Surrey, the Mole flows on past Dorking, Leatherhead, and Cobham, and then taking its leave of bold hills and rich woods, and ancestral mansions, it hastens through the flat region of the Moulseys towards the Thames. Much has been written both in poetry and prose upon the Mole, and many are the landscapes that other artists besides Witherington have painted near its tranquil waters. As late as the time of the lordly builder of Hampton Court, known as the "Emlay," this river has both changed its name and acquired its celebrity from the singular circumstance of its underground excesses; but I must be compelled to state that, though there is some cause to call it subterranean, yet the poets have grievously exaggerated truth. Spencer tells us that

"The Mole doth make
His way still under ground, till Thames he overtake."

Drayton declares that the Mole

"Underneath the earth for three miles space doth creep."

Milton calls it

"The sullen Mole that runneth underneath."

and Pope avows that he

"Hides his diving flood."

When to these poetical licenses Camden has attached

his staider prose, stating that "the inhabitants of this tract, no less than the Spaniards, may boast of a bridge that feeds several flocks of sheep." Without doubt, wonder-seekers will meet with little but disappointment if they raise their expectations by crediting such faithless oracles. The plain fact is, that, in the neighbourhood of Box Hill and Norbury Park, the bed of the stream is composed of a very porous earth, in which, at some little depth below the surface, many cavernous hollows are supposed to have been formed. In ordinary seasons the supply of water is sufficient, as well to fill these hidden recessess as to maintain a stream on the surface; not so however, in any time of drought; then the stream entirely fails, and for some distance the channel is perfectly dry. Near the bridge at Thorncroft the ground again becomes solid, and here accordingly the exhausted river rises in a strong spring, and resumes its original condition. As it will be readily supposed, this singular interruption in the course of the Mole, gave rise at early periods, to a variety of marvellous legends; but as to any picturesque "diving" headlong into the bowels of the earth, or any open and avowed tendency to emulate in Plutonic shades, Lethe, Cocytus, or Avernus, let none but poets expect a wonder so ideal. There is a very elaborate map of this same river Mole, published in London, which I have seen, and in this is marked down every hole and swallow in its course with great accuracy, thus demonstrating how its waters waste away.

Few think our own river Alun is of so much importance as to be reckoned with these two great rivers, to share with them this most singular characteristic; but so it is—its course can be traced to where it leaves mother earth's surface, thence where it again returns to hail the light, running, as it does, at this portion of its career, over a bed of lime-stone rock, it is absorbed by what is known frequently to occur in lime-stone mountains, namely, large natural caverns; or, as these are termed in mining operations, "swallows." This part of the country is peculiar for containing very many of these swallows, which, to a great extent, obstruct the working in a proper way, the lead mines in this mountain. Now, it is a pity to destroy so great a curiosity as this peculiar course of the River Alun, even in thought; but it has often occurred to me that, as this underground stream of the Alun is little more than half a mile, and as it is known to do so great a mischief as to prevent the proper following the mineral veins, is it not feasible to cut a new channel on the surface, away from the neighbourhood of the mines, and turn its stream from feeding all these swallows: thus, by cutting off the supply, render it possible in time to pump these swallows dry, and follow the lodes of lead to where they now lead below this " waste of waters."

But I am afraid I am getting out of my depth; so let us return to the surface, for we are in a wild country now, about two miles from Cilcen; so set we our faces homewards; and though we have many a rood of waste-like ground to traverse ere we gain pleasant Mold, still, let us reflect how much health and wealth, and homestead happiness, shines perennially from the face of beautiful Flintshire, beaming up with gratitude to God; and though, in truth, we have our share of barrenness, and desolation in the parts where we are now wandering, in many a broad strip of moorland, still, how fresh and fair are our downs and heaths, and far-stretching lines of hills—how rich and Eden-like our valleys, how stately our ancestral woods, how trim our cottage gardens, how fertile our soil in grain and roots and luscious fruits, how rich in mineral treasures our mountains, how various in all kinds of beauty, and of interest, and of wealth, is this full theme of Flintshire. And, hark! what is that comes cheerily on this scene where we thought we were wandering in silence and loneliness? 'Tis the sweet voice of innocent childhood being dismissed from the school at Gwernaffield.

You must have perceived during the progress of this lecture, that my desire has been to gossip with my audience now and then, believing that matters of fact are rendered more impressive by indulgence in those fancies which are suggested by scenes and incidents described; so this interruption in our quiet progress by "the noisy children just let loose from school," naturally suggests a comparison between the venerable adjunct of the village in old times, and that by which it is now-a-days usually "adorned."

There are few things so changed in character throughout Britain, both internally and externally, as its village schools, which, in days not long gone by, were nearest in picturesque effect to the village church—simple contemplative dwellings, covered with climbers, coronetted with flowers, a many-paned window at either side of the door, which was shaded by a covered porch, sometimes solid and thatched, or else open and matted with woodbine: this terminated the path whose line was carefully marked out and guarded by a border of thrift or a box edging, while within the sanctury flourished all kinds of "poseys," wallflowers, and stocks, and sweet-williams, and riband-grass, a white rose and a red rose bush; and, mayhap, a flaunting York and Lancaster rose, or a tower of white lilies—the gift of sweet "Miss Mary," who married, had children, five, and now is in the church-yard, underneath an altar-tomb,—herb rosemary grew there, and woody lavender, and lavender cotton.

> "The tufted basil, pun-provoking thyme
> Fresh baum, and marigold of cheerful hue."

and streaky pinks, and rich crimson cloves, and sage, (a leaf in tea to make it wholesome), and feathery fennel, and such hot turnip radishes, and little onions, whose silver bulbs disdained the earth, and shot their waving green and narrow leaves above their heads; the row of double parsley was a green banquet to the eye. All was in harmony with the sweet low-roofed house, from which came the hum of young voices, sometimes low and sweet, sometimes shrill and troubled. The low palings, which divided the garden from the road, were green from age, and had as it were, taken root and grown their own way—some remaining upright in their rectitude of purpose; others, like weak-minded persons, leaning to the right or left, and having no will of their own. Often a black-bird or a thrush hung in a wicker cage beneath the porch; an old tom-cat on the window-sill winked at the sun-beams, and beyond, close to the yew hedge, whose centre was clipped into some monstrosity called a "pea-cock," or "flower-pot," lay a shelf of bee-hives, more than half concealed from public gaze by a row of broad beans or blossoming peas, upon which the bees under the straw thatch came to banquet.

Now, the school house is generally a new clean trim two-storied house, of no particular order of architecture; but upon the external ornamentation of which, enough has been spent, to clothe, as well as to educate, a rising generation. Money, it has been said, is not wealth: neither is size, or elaboration, beauty; and, as yet, our national schools look hard and dictatorial. When the softening hand of time passes over those seats of embryo learning—when the bright red brick, or the pure white stone is toned down by the weather, and ivy and virginia-creeper clasp the gables, and take off the sharpness of those corners—when, in fact, the new becomes the old—

the schools of the present time will better harmonise with the character of our beloved British scenery.

But, if the change is so apparent in the schools, what is it in the teachers? Shenstone has drawn with fidelity the picture of the "dame," in the old times of dames' schools:—

> "Her cap far whiter than the driven snow,
> Emblem right meet of decency does yield:
> Her apron dyed in grain—as blue I trow,
> As is the harebell that adorns the field;
> And in her hand, for sceptre she does wield
> Tway birchen sprays."

She was old and mild, but firm; the nod was her help, the rod was her argument; the shake was her warning, the fool's cap her disgrace; a kind smile or word, accompanied by a gingerbread nut on rare occasions, her reward.

We cannot but wonder how those bright cleverlooking women, sent from normal schools, to diffuse education in our country parishes, would look in close mob-caps, whiter than the driven snow, linsey aprons, and "russet stoles and kirtles!" Alas? for the back-of-the-head bonnets and gay muslin—I beg pardon, gay *mousseline*—dresses that sweep the school-room floors, and the air of superiority with which our simple questions, born of domestic wants, are often answered—making us sigh for the days when girls were taught by dames to mend stockings, darn invisibly, sew on buttons—to remain on—and piece linen or broadcloth so that the rent became a myth.

And now, you will perceive, we are drawing near home, and nearer to the bright particular spot I wish to bestow some thoughtful consideration upon, namely, the well-known event in early history called the "Alleluia victory."

And here, as we traverse the very ground this struggle occurred upon, it would be unpardonable in an essay like the present, not to give it a full consideration; so we will turn to the right when we are opposite the gateway leading to the house of Rhual, and enter the field opposite that gateway, known as the "Obelisk Field," from the memorial placed in it to commemorate this battle; and there, looking on the same face of nature these hostile armies gazed upon, and treading the same ground where they encamped, bring back, in memory, the events that occured fourteen centuries ago.

I approach the subject I now purpose introducing, with much diffidence, conscious that not a few will be apt to consider it highly presumptuous on my part daring to propound theories, or offer explanations of circumstances that happened so many centuries since, and on the very spot where they took place, and I a stranger in the land. But, perhaps, that very circumstance may conduce to your hearing an impartial opinion; and, at the best, how can we show our knowledge of these events but by the facts recorded in history, which, happily, is now so

MAESGARMON, MOLD.
(The Bailey Hill and Church in the Distance.)

well known, that it is impossible to pervert facts without being controverted; and it is only by a careful arrangement of facts, and weighing their effects, that we can expect to arrive at anything like a true exposition of our subject. We all know, from tradition, that a great defeat was sustained by an invading enemy upon the ground we are now supposed to be traversing, and so important was it deemed, that, until the present time, it has retained the memory of the event in the names given to the district: but of the causes of that invasion, and the state of society at the time, which contributed to its defeat, few turn their thoughts; and to the task of describing some of these circumstances I purpose briefly to attempt. And in starting, let me premise with a few observations, which may be thought irrelevant by some, but which I hope will be deemed a sufficient excuse by the many, for going so far back in time for the illustration of our subject.

To trace it clearly, we must begin with the days of Druidism in this country; and it is a remarkable fact, that from all the narratives given of the conquest of this island by the Romans, none expressly mention the existence of Druidism in any other part of the British Isles but Anglesea. If the matter depended entirely on the testimony of the Greek and Roman writers, the common opinion would scarcely rest on sufficient grounds. But the general prevalence of Druidism in Britain, appears to be abundantly established, both by the material monuments of that system of religion which are spread over all parts of the country, and by popular customs and superstitions derived from the same source which have either survived to our own day, or have only recently disappeared. Such, in passing, let me observe, that the practice of the Druidical worship appears to have subsisted among the people long after the Druids as an order of priesthood were extinct. The annals of the sixth, seventh, and even of the eighth century, contain numerous edicts of emperors, and canons of councils, against the worship of the sun, the moon, mountains, rivers, lakes, and trees. There is even a law to the same effect of the English king Canute, in the eleventh century. Nor, as I before had occasion to remark, have some of the practices of the old superstition yet altogether ceased to be remembered in our popular sports, pastimes, and anniversary usages. The ceremonies of All-Hallowmass, or Nos Galen, the bonfires of May-day and Mid-summer Eve, the virtues attributed to the mistletoe in our Christmas pastimes, and various other customs of the villages and the country parts of, as well here, as in England, Scotland, and Ireland; still speak to us of the days of Druidism. And who here but must have noticed in our fairs, the buyers and sellers of the cattle, reaching out their hands to each other when making or concluding a bargain, thinks that it is an important rite of Druidism. It is recorded by an author whom I have consulted on several occasions in this notice of Druidism, that when the Druidical system of priesthood was giving place to Christianity, "there were some practices of Druidical origin allowed to remain, and recognised by the law of the land even when others, more strictly evangelical, had been introduced. Such was the mode of joining hand in hand in swearing, which the code of Hywel Dda authorised in certain cases, as those of buying and selling." All this will evince that the impression of its grim ritual has not been wholly obliterated from the popular imagination by the lapse of nearly twenty centuries.

It is with the Britons of the south exclusively that we are concerned, for among these only have we reason to believe that any kind of learning or scientific knowledge existed at the time to which this enquiry relates. Among the south Britons, there was undoubtedly established a class of persons, forming a clergy, not only in the modern, but in the original, and more extensive signification of the term; that is to say, a body of national functionaries, intrusted with the superintendence over all the departments of learning. The Druids were not merely their theologians and priests, but their lawyers, their physicians, their teachers of youth, their moral and natural philosophers, their astronomers, their mathematicians, their architects, their musicians, their poets, and in that character no doubt, also, their only historians. To them, in short, were left the care and control of the whole intellectual culture of the nation.

It is most probable that, in discharging this duty, the Druids proceeded upon the principle of imparting none of their knowledge except to such as they trained up to be members of their own body. The state of society would scarcely admit of any diffusion of their knowledge among the people at large, and the genius of their system, as far as it can be detected, appears to have been wholly opposed to any such lavish communication of that to which they owed all their ascendancy over their fellow-countrymen. To them knowledge was power, not only in the sense in which it is so to every individual in the possession of it, as enabling him to do those things, the way of doing which it teaches, but besides, and to a much larger extent, as putting into their hands an instrument of authority and command over all around them.

The Druidical clergy appear to have been a body of the same sort with the clergy of any modern Christian church ; that is to say, consisting, not of the members of particular families, but of persons educated to the profession from any of all the families in the land. It may be assumed, however, that they were principally derived from the more opulent or honourable classes. Cæsar describes the young men who—some of their own accord, others sent by their friends and relations—resorted to the Druids of

Gaul to obtain instruction in their system, and to be trained to become members of their body, as very numerous. Pomponius Mela speaks of their pupils as consisting of the most noble individuals of the nation.

In regard to the particular studies in which these crowds of pupils were exercised, our information, as might be expected, is very unsatisfactory. Both Cæsar and Mela state the fact of their sometimes remaining twenty years under tuition; and the former reports that they were said, in the course of that time, to learn a great number of verses. The consecration of poetry for the diffusion and transmission of truth, was an extremely wise and prudent measure. Verse is quickly and easily learned; its influence over the feelings is great; it dwells long on the memory; and from the nature of its structure, almost defies perversion.

The art of eloquence was no doubt assiduously cultivated, and held in the highest honour, both by the Druids, and by the other leading personages among the Celtic nations. In the state of society which then subsisted, this was the most powerful instrument for ruling the popular mind, as it still is among the Islanders of the South Sea and the Indians of America in a much less advanced social condition. Among both the Gauls and the Britons we read of displays of oratory in all their public proceedings. The debates of their councils, and the direction of their armies, alike demanded the exercise of this popular accomplishment. The harangues delivered on certain memorable occasions by Galgacus, Caractacus, Boadicea, and other British chiefs have been preserved to us by the Roman writers. Tacitus has depicted the Druids of Mona, when that sanctuary was attacked by the Roman general Suetonius, rushing, with burning torches outstretched before them, through the ranks of their armed countrymen arrayed to repel the invaders, and inflaming their courage by pouring forth frenzied prayers with their hands uplifted to heaven. On other occasions, according to Diodorus Siculus, they would evince their powers of persuasion by throwing themselves between two bodies of combatants, ready to engage; and by the charm of their words, as if by enchantment, appeasing their mutual rage, and prevailing upon them to throw down their arms. In the administration of the laws, also, and in the celebration of their religious solemnities, they would, no doubt, often have occasion to address the people. The artificial mounts called Carnedds, still remaining in Anglesey, and in other parts of Wales, are supposed to have formed the stations from which they were wont to deliver their regular instructions and admonitions to the listening crowd. On the whole, shrouded from our distinct view as the facts of the subject are by the remoteness of the time, and the scantiness of the light shed upon them by history, there is reason to believe that these studious Celtic priests had accumulated no contemptible stock of knowledge in various departments of science and philosophy. According to Ammianus Marcellinus, it was to the Druids that the Gauls were indebted for nearly all that they possessed of civilization and learning; and the same thing, in all probability, might have been said of the Britons.

That with the real and valuable knowledge possessed by the Druids, there was much error and superstition mixed up, there can be no doubt; everything they believed, and everything they taught may have been, at the best, but a mixture of truth and falsehood; but still it would be very far from being worthless on that account.

In the most advanced state to which human knowledge has yet attained, it has, perhaps, in no department, been purified from all alloy of error; and in the greater number of the fields of philosophical speculation, the conjectural and the doubtful still form a large portion of the most successful investigations that the wit of man has been able to achieve. Civilization could never make any progress, if nothing except knowledge, free from all error, could carry it forward.

One result of the Roman invasion of Britain was, the introduction into the island of the Christian faith. An event so important might be expected to hold a prominent place in our early chronicles. The missionary by whom Christianity was first brought to this island, the manner in which it was impressed upon the belief of so primitive a people, and the persons by whom its profession was earliest adopted, are particulars which it would have been interesting and gratifying to find recorded. But from the obscurity that pervades the ecclesiastical records of the first century, and the unobstrusive silence with which the commencing steps of the Christian faith were made, it cannot be accounted strange if Britain, a country at that time so remote and insignificant, should have the beginning of her religious history involved in much obscurity. The investigations of the curious, however, have, partly by bold conjectures, and partly from monkish legends, attempted to show how Britain either was, or might have been, Christianized. But rejecting suppositions, all that can be regarded as well established is, that at a comparatively early period, Christianity found its way into the British islands. The path once opened, and the work commenced, successive missionaries would follow to extend the sphere of action and increase the number of the converts. Circumstances too, were peculiarly favourable in Britain for a successful progress. The preceding subtle and influential priesthood of Druidism, who might have the most effectually opposed the new faith, had been early destroyed by the swords of the conquerors;

and the latter were too intent upon achieving the complete subjection of the country, to concern themselves about the transition of the inhabitants from one system of religious opinions to another. A passing allusion, in the writings of Tertullian, gives us a more distinct idea of the state of Christianity in Britain, than can be obtained from any narratives of the monastic writers of the times. In his work against the Jews, written A.D. 209, he says that "even those places in Britain hitherto inaccessible to the Roman arms have been subdued by the Gospel of Christ."

As yet, the remoteness of Britain, and the suppression of the Druids, had equally preserved its humble church from foreign and domestic persecution; but the time arrived when it was to share in those afflictions which fell to the lot of the Christian world at large. Diocletian, inspired with hatred and jealousy at the predominance of doctrines which were supposed to menace all civil authority, addressed himself to the entire destruction of Christianity; and edicts were published in every part of the Roman empire for the suppression of its rites and the persecution of its followers. In a storm so universal, Britain was no longer overlooked; and St. Alban, the first martyr of our island, perished, with many others whose names have not been recorded. This event, according to the venerable Bede, took place in the year 286; but if it really happened in the great persecution under Diocletian, a date at least seventeen or eighteen years later must be assigned to it. Although Constantius, who, at this time, directed the affairs of Britain, was favourably inclined towards the Christians, he durst not oppose the imperial mandate; and however he might indirectly alleviate its severities, yet the inferior magistrates had no such scruples.

One incident at this time, as related by Eusebius, betrayed his friendly disposition towards the persecuted. Assembling the officers of his household, he announced to them the pleasure of the Emperor, requiring the dismission of the Christians from office, and gave those who were of that religion their choice either to renounce their creed or resign their situations. Some of them, unwilling to make the required sacrifice, abjured their faith, upon which Constantius discharged them from his service, declaring that, those who had renounced their God could never prove true to a master. But this persecution, which had almost extinguished the Christian faith, subsided as suddenly as it had commenced, and the British church was restored to its former tranquillity. Of the history of Christianity in our islands during the third century we know little or nothing. From the time of the accession of Constantine, however, in the beginning of the fourth century, the hitherto secluded church of Britain seems to have become united to the civilised world, and to have been considered as making a part of the spiritual empire which he established.

After the Christian church had been established in power and splendour, the same results were exhibited in Britain as in other countries; and while the Italian and Greek infused into the Christian faith the classical Paganism of his fathers, the Briton leavened it with his ancestral Druidical superstitions. About the beginning of the fifth century the internal peace of the church of Britain was first disturbed by the introduction of the errors of Pelagius. This heretic was a native of Britain; his original name was Morgan, which, in Welsh, means "near the Sea." Pelagius, a Greek word adopted by the Romans, has the same signification; it is generally supposed he was educated at the monastery of Bangor Iscoed, in Flintshire; but this has been disputed, many averring he was educated at Bangor, or Banchor, near Carrickfergus in Ireland, where he met his disciple and coadjutor Celestius, who has always been claimed as an Irishman. About the end of the fourth century he quitted the land of his birth, and in the company of Celestius travelled to Rome, where they began to propound principles which affected the Catholic doctrine of original sin and divine grace. About A.D. 410 they left Rome, and after a variety of wanderings in Europe and Africa—everywhere disseminating these theories—which, from their daring variety, and the attractive form in which the preachers addressed their multitudes of hearers—for Celestius is every where allowed to have been a man of great subtilty and readiness of wit—caused great schisms among the faithful; the arch-heretics were summoned before an august council held at Carthage, and there both the eastern and western churches were unanimous in their condemnation of those doctrines which had already unsettled the faith of thousands in Christendom. In addition to this, the Emperors Honorius and Theodosius issued their decrees, whereby both Pelagius and Celestius, with their followers, were formally banished from the Roman dominions. The principal opponents of the Welshman and his disciples were Saints Jerome and Augustine—great names, certainly; but we hope the controversy was carried on in a less bitter spirit than we learn from the writings of the saint which have come down to us; for Saint Jerome in one of his passionate invectives, calls Celestius a blockhead, swollen with Scotch pottage; that is, what we should now call Irish flummery. The original Latin is *Scotorum pultibus prægravatus.* I may quote as a specimen of the eloquence of the age, and also of its most orthodox Christianity, a little more of the splended bile of the learned saint. He goes on to describe Celestius as "a great corpulent barking dog, fitter to kick with his heels than to bite with his teeth; a Cerberus, who, with his master Pluto," (so Pelagius is designated) "deserved to be knocked on the head, and so put to eternal silence." Saint Augustine, however, is far less rancorous, for he has spoke most energetically as to Pelagius's moral character and piety.

On the other hand, he found an able advocate in John, patriarch of Jerusalem, and also in his successor Prailius, and both Innocent and Zozimus, the Roman pontiffs, were his friends.

The Pelagian heresy, as I have before intimated, consisted mainly in a denial of original sin, and of the necessity of divine grace to perform good works. These tenets, so agreeable to human nature, gained, as might be expected, many converts, even after their authors had been silenced. Their progress in Gaul was so rapid and extensive as to induce the emperor Valentinian, A.D. 425, to issue his mandate to Patroclus, archbishop of Arles, enjoining him to convene all the bishops who entertained them; and provided they did not recant within twenty days they were forthwith to be banished the country. It is supposed that in consequence of this edict, many came over to Britain, and amongst them Agricola, son of bishop Severianus, who is mentioned as the first who taught Pelagianism among the people of this land. It is natural to think they had many followers, for the fame of Pelagius's virtues and talents would alone recommend his tenets to the particular notice of his enthusiastic countrymen. We must also recollect that most, if not all, of the Cambrian clergy were bards; and that some of the theories of Pelagius, about the freedom of the will, agreed essentially with certain exploded maxims of Druidism. Nevertheless, the leading ecclesiastics adhered steadfastly to "the faith which was once delivered to the saints," though for obvious reasons, they were not sufficiently learned to confute the subtle propositions of their adversaries. They therefore applied for assistance to their more experienced brethren in Gaul. It was A.D. 429, that a synod of Gallican prelates was convened, in which the case of the applicants was taken into consideration, and it was determined that Garmon, (Germanus) bishop of Auxerre, and Bleiddian, (Lupus) bishop of Troyes, should both forthwith visit Britain in person. Garmon was of Welsh extraction, being the son of Rhidyw, and uncle of Emyr Llydaw, an Armorican prince, and on that account was much better qualified for the object he had in view than if he had been a stranger to the language of the Country. These "apostolical priests." as they are styled by Constantius, on their arrival in Britain, applied themselves to their appointed task with great zeal and devotion. They preached in the churches and fields and highways, with such success, that multitudes of the heterodox were convinced, and the weak and wavering confirmed on all sides. The heads of the heresy having at first kept out of the way, were at length compelled, by a sense of shame or despair, to meet their antagonists, and discuss the merits of their different tenets at a public conference.

The Pelagian teachers, according to the narrative of the venerable Bede, came to the arena in great pomp, and advocated their cause with the most showy rhetoric; but Germanus and Lupus, when it was their turn to reply, entered on the confutation with a wonderful force of rhetoric, reason, and scripture proof, and so overwhelmed them with arguments and authorities, owned their being baffled by not answering. The venerable historian who relates this conference seems quite to revel in his statement of their discomfiture. He says "as for the people, they gave sentence in their acclamations; they shouted for Germanus and Lupus, and could scarce command their temper so far as to forbear beating the Pelagians." But Bede was too orthodox and too credulous to have doubted the tradition, if it had affirmed that the arguments of the Gallic bishops on this occasion had struck their antagonists dead as well as dumb.

It was at about this conjuncture of affairs that there appear in North Britain two powerful and distinct tribes, who are not before mentioned in history. These were the Picts and Scots. The name of the former people has caused much but seemingly unnecessary speculation. The Picts seem to have been that race of free Britons beyond the Roman wall who retained the habit of staining the body when going into battle, and were called by the Romans and Roman colonists, the painted men. Claudian proves that these natives actually followed the custom of painting their bodies, as implied by the expression—*nec falso nomine Pictos*—"nor falsely termed the Picts."

The Scots, on the other hand, were of Irish origin; for, to the great confusion of ancient history, the inhabitants of Ireland—those at least of the conquering and predominating caste—were called Scots. These two free nations of Picts and Scots appear to have resembled each other in manner and ferocity, and to have exercised the last quality without scruple on the Roman colonists. War was their sole pursuit, slaughter their chief delight; their worship might be termed that of demons, since the imaginary beings whom they adored, were the personification of their own evil pursuits and passions, so it was no wonder they worshipped the imaginary god of battle with barbarous and inhuman rites. We have a palpable instance that these Pictish rovers were strangers to the doctrines of Christianity, and opposed to the sacred cause of learning and religion, in the demolition of the college or monastery of Caerworgan, in South Wales, and the capture of its principal. But He, whose providence brings good out of evil, converted this calamity into a real blessing for the Irish nation at large, for the person carried away by the depredators was none other than the great St. Patrick himself. Thus, even over this wild people, the Sun of Righteousness arose with healing under his wings. Good men, on whom the name of saint was justly bestowed, to whom life and the pleasures of this world were as nothing, so they could call souls to Christianity, undertook and succeeded in the perilous task of enlightening these savages.

The conference which I have described between the Pelagian teachers and the orthodox champions Garmon and Bleiddian, was held at Verulam, the present St. Albans, then one of the most important cities of Britain. After the victory they there achieved, they travelled about preaching, and rendering great aid to the British church. Much is related of them by Bede and other early writers; but the most important particular of their labours which concerns us, is the miraculous defeat of the enemy upon the ground where we are now supposed to be resting. I purpose being as concise as possible in the relatian of this event; but I must enter into particulars because it has occasioned some controversy among eminent writers. We are told that, during the time these pious bishops were journeying through the island, "the Saxons and Picts, with their united forces, made war upon the Britons." Now much talent and ingenuity has been exerted by the Rev. Mr. Whitaker, in the attempt to disprove altogether the account of the Hallelujah victory. He founds his objections principally upon what appear to be some chronological and other errors in the statement of Constantius and Bede. He says we cannot for instance find any reason for believing that the Saxons invaded Britain so early, or that they made war in conjunction with the Picts. But it is evident from several authorities that the Britons had been disturbed by Saxon parties before the time of Hengist. Ammianus Marcellinus informs us it was so in the reign of Valentinian 1st, and Claudian introduces the Saxons, Picts, and Scots together, where Britain is making panegyric upon Stilichon; and it appears from the Notitia Imperii that a "comes Saxonici littoris" had been expressly appointed by the Romans to guard the British coasts against this foreign enemy. Archbishop Usher also further informs us that the spot bore the name of Maes Garmon in his day, and had so done as long as tradition could be traced; and the learned prelate was much struck with the coincidence, and he wrote more than 200 years ago. Considering the testimony on which the account rests it seems, in substance, to be satisfactorily accredited. Besides, it is very probable that, instead of "Saxons and Picts," we ought to read "Scots and Picts."

I shall confine myself to Bede's narrative, who says, the Britons, thinking themselves unequal to their enemies, implored the assistance of the holy bishops. The latter hastening to them, inspired them with so much courage, that they felt as though they had been joined by a mighty army. The days of Lent were also at hand, which would be rendered more solemn by the presence of the priests; the people resorted in crowds to be baptized, most of the army desiring also to participate in that rite. A church was prepared for that purpose of interwoven branches of trees, which we know from tradition and authorities was the practice of first founding churches in these early days. The spot thus made sacred was termed "Llan," and the church bore the name of its holy founder; so by this we know the exact spot where the British army encamped, and where this baptism took place, namely, Llanarmon. These churches could not be supposed to last long thus constructed; but they were readily made to serve their purpose at first, and were afterwards more solidly constructed of split trees; for, strange as it may appear, although the Britons must have been well skilled in the working of stones, as the Druidical remains to this day testify, yet none of their early churches were of aught but wood; and this was the same in other portions of the island, for Bede mentions that Finan, being ordained by the Scots to succeed Aidan in his bishopric, built in the island of Lindisfarne, a church fit for an episcopal see, of sawn timber, covering it with reeds. The most extraordinary existing instance of such a primitive British church is at Greensted, in Essex, which is believed to have been originally erected in haste to receive the body of the martyr king, St. Edmund, in its passage from Suffolk to London. The body of the church is formed by a series of split trees, the flat side inward, and the rough bark outward; they fit in sockets above and below, also formed of timber.

But to proceed with our narrative from Bede.—"The enemy received advice of the state of the army and, not questioning their success against such a mob, hastened forward; but their approach was, by the scouts, made known to the Britons, and Garmon declared he would be their leader. He picked out the most active, moved forward from where they were then posted, and passing along a country by the way the enemy was expected, where was a number of small valleys surrounded by low hills, there he drew up his inexperienced troops, himself acting as their general."

"And soon a multitude of fierce enemies appear; Garmon, bearing in his hands the standard, instructed the men all in a loud voice to repeat his words. The enemy advancing securely as thinking to take them by surprise, the priests three times cried Alleluia! Alleluia! Alleluia! a universal shout of the same word followed, and the hills resounded with an echo on all sides." There can be little doubt but Garmon calculated on the effect of this echo; for as the troops marched from Llanarmon, their road lay past Aberdûne, where is a fine natural echo. He would find as great an echo within about a hundred yards of where the farm house of Maesgarmon now stands, a man of his great talents would know how to take advantage of this natural phenomenon; hence it is not wonderful that we read that "the enemy was struck with dread, fearing, that not only the neighbouring hills, but the very skies were falling upon them."

And now, in another shape, nature was helping the Britons, for during the time their enemies were advancing, after having crossed the River Alun, there fell heavy torrents of rain. And who among us, has not observed in these days the effect of a continuous rain, for even so short a period as of one revolution of the earth on its axis, on the meadows above Rhydgaled; and what would it be in these early days, when artificial draining was never dreamed of, when rivers flowed through primeval forests, often with no visible banks, extending their waters for miles through a jungle of underwood, involving the land in an unsuccessful attempt to keep its head above the water. In such a state, perhaps, the low-lying valley, between what is now, Rhual on the one side, and Llwynegrin on the other, was at that time, when the invaders feet were not swift enough to deliver them from their terror, it was more a rout than a panic; they turned from their foes, and found a worse foe in front—a land that would look as if, in the early stages, of either being submerged by the flood, or draining off after it. Poor untutored savages, showing no mercy, therefore expecting none, rushing headlong into the troubled waters, heaps upon heaps, the only feeling to get out of the reach of their pursuers, and yet going to quicker destruction as each lost his footing in the stream, catching at the nearest man to him; scores locked thus together, and thus impeding each ones free movement, making their death by drowning even more sure; and when by chance any found footing, their opponents, ready with stones and other missiles, to hurl at him and destroy all chance of escape, and plenty of missiles were at hand; for Bede tells us that in their flight they cast away their arms, hoping with their naked bodies to escape the danger. The Britons, without the loss of a single man, beheld their vengeance complete; and, after gathering up the scattered spoils, rejoiced in the success which Heaven had granted them.

I may have appeared tedious ; but my purpose would not have been obtained had I been less circumstantial. All who have heard me will at least understand the important part this little spot around Mold occupies in the "History of the religion of Ancient Britain." Both writers and readers of history form an unworthy estimate of its province if they restrict it to a bare recital of events. They only realise its mission who see in its transitions the successive developements of Providence, ever working without pause and without failure, the council of the Divine will. It is not enough if we would study history aright, that we should follow in the track of battle, and listen to the wail of the vanquished and to the shouts of conquerors ; it is not enough that we should philosophically analyze the causes of upheaval and remodelling ; it is not enough that we regard it as a school for the study of character, and gaze with an admiration that is almost awe upon "the world's foster gods," the stalwart nobility of mankind ; it is not enough that we should regard it as a chaos of incident, "a mighty maze and all without a plan ;" we realise the true ideal of history only when we discover God in it, shaping its ends for the evolution of His own design, educing order from its vast confusions, resolving its complications into one grand and marvellous unity, and making it a body of completeness and symmetry, with himself as the informing soul.

Let this faith be fastened on our spirits, and history becomes a beautiful study. There is sure warrant for the expectation of that progress of which the poetwatchers have so hopefully sung; progress unintermitting, through every disaster of the past, heralding progress, yet diviner, in every possibility of the future. The eye of sense may trace but scanty foreshadowings of the brightness; there may be dark omens in the aspect of the times—clouds may gather gloomily around, and the wistful glance, strained through the darkness, may discern but faint traces of the coming of the day; but it shall come, and every moment brings it nigher—for "the word of the Lord hath spoken it," and that word "endureth for ever."

And now we pass the foot of the Baily Hill, what a history that could tell had we time to relate its story; of the castle which stood on its summit, its garrisons, its sieges, its battles, and its slain; hardly comprehensible at the present day, when we look in vain for a single stone as a memorial that it once existed.

Time, the never resting, presses stealthily onward, and tells me I must now close my tour round Mold, finishing my pleasant task, hopeful that my hearers have shared with me the enjoyment I have so long and so often derived from my walks round my adopted home. I have traced one side of the beautiful valley in a circuit of about twelve miles, and in our walk have shown how rich it is in antiquarian, legendary, geological, and historical lore; yet my object has not been answered if I have failed to show, that, although in landscape beauty it may be inferior to many other valleys—its natural graces and scenic grandeur less, the vale of Mold has attractions of its own, which place it high above many competitors. It is a pleasant task, and brings with it a large reward, that which has for its aim and end to make manifest the advantages that recompense a home tour. It is in the power of any author, no matter how humble, who writes of Britain, to show how manifold are its means to create enjoyment, to convey instruction, and to augment a national pride of country, that instinctive patriotism which, without contracting the heart or narrowing the mind, leads to faith in one's own as the best. Several circumstances have of late combined to induce acquaintance with the charms of scenery, grand or beautiful which our islands so plentifully supply. The lonely lakes, the mountain rocks that guard our coasts, the rugged mountains, the wood-clad hills, the dense forests, the delicious dells, the rippling burns, the rapid rivers, the spacious harbours, the green islets, the rural villages, the luxurious demesnes—these and a thousand other charms await the traveller, who journeys through any of the shires of Wales, England, Scotland, or Ireland. Scenes that are associated with glorious memories are wholesome and honourable stimulants; such places are found in our own land, where every step is a reminder that we live in a free country, under the sway of a sovereign, to whom every subject of every degree, while rendering obedience as a sacred duty, offers the homage of the heart. This imperfect notice is evidence, which justifies all who honor

"The venerable name of our adored country"

in exclaiming with the poet

"O, thou Queen,
Thou delegated Deity of earth
O dear, dear Britain!"

THE preceding remarks embody the observations made by, and the impressions derived from, certain walks round Mold, of an ardent lover of Nature.

But it will be observed they refer to one side only of the Town and its River; he leaves to future tourists the task of recording their remarks upon what may be found on the other side of the circle—for strolls through the townships of Gwysaney, Argoed and Bistree, will produce as much legendary lore, and afford as beautiful scenic views as the places noticed in the foregoing Rambles.

Continuation of the Rambles.

IN the Preface to the preceding pages, the publishers of this work speak of their intention of adding such descriptive and statistical details as are required to give the work the character it assumes to be, namely, a guide book to the town and neighbourhood; they must however commence with stating, they will enter into no history of the place, but only go back to the period that may be remembered by the present generation, and first as to the improvements and additions in the town itself.

Most of the present inhabitants remember the old building at the Cross, in which the judges used to meet to hold the county assize; this building was private property, belonging in fact to the lord of the manor, in which in its original state, it was dedicated to the holding, what were termed, court leets; but its dilapidated condition at length compelled the magistrates to find better accommodation wherein public justice could be administered, not however until it had become so ruinous, that the judges, sometimes, when the weather was rainy, would feel the rain dripping through the roof on to their heads as they sat on the bench; for two judges went the circuit at that time, and stayed always a full week at Tymawr in Mold.

Until the old building was pulled down there stood on the north side of it, that oft-noticed relic of olden discipline, the Parish Stocks. The present writer cannot say he ever saw it used for its legitimate purpose; but one piece of barbarism he well recollects having seen enforced in the high street of Mold, that is, a man flogged on his bare back, from the Bailey Hill to the Cross, fastened by his hands to the back of a cart, the horse attached to which, trotted at a sharp pace down the street, while the prisoner was forced to run at the same pace, the executioner with his whip following in a like run, all the while using his whip on the man's back.

In the year 1833 it was determined to use the old Hall no longer, and the result was, the present County Hall rose in its stead; but even this solid looking building was likely to come to grief, for soon after its completion, an enterprising individual opened the ground within a few yards of its walls and sank a shaft to seek for coal, which he found; but unfortunately the seam ran in the direction of the ground under the foundation of the building, and when removed the ground above of course gave way, the result was, one morning the hall itself was found to be cracked and twisted in an alarming manner, threatening its complete destruction; the first thing done was to stop the workings underneath, and shore up the ground, the next to look to the building.

It had at this time a very elegant gothic lantern in the centre of the roof, rising up to the height of about twenty feet, in the form of a church spire, this it was found imperative to remove, to lighten the walls; then with screws and other appliances the walls were held together, until iron rods and braces were introduced, and this has been so far effective that no other displacement has since been observed, and in this state is the County Hall tied together to this day.

An action was brought against the parties who had caused the injuries, but nothing came of it, for not until then did it transpire that when the county authorities bought the ground to build the hall upon, they had only purchased the surface, the mineral right having been bought by the parties who opened the ground to get at the coal.

Soon after the old leet hall was sold to a joint-stock company, called the "Mold Market Company," who pulled it down in 1849, and erected on its site the handsome and commodious building now standing at the Cross, the ground floor being appropriated to market stalls, chiefly butchers, the upper floor containing two spacious assembly rooms. This building is one of the largest of its kind in Wales. The rooms over the market space being used for Concerts, Assemblies, Lectures, and indeed for any purpose where it is necessary to accommodate large assemblages of people under cover, and they have always been found to be sufficiently spacious. A unique instance of their usefulness has lately been shewn, in being called into requisition to accommodate a company of military, and here it may be as well to record the cause that brought regular soldiers to preserve the peace of, otherwise, quiet Mold.

At Leeswood Green Colliery near to Mold a large number of men are employed, and these having some objection to one of their underground agents refused to obey his rule, and were determined to get rid of him. On the 19th of May, 1869, they forcibly expelled him from his home, even going so far as to break into his house and carry all his household goods to the railway station; eight of the rioters were arrested and some committed for trial. During the trial a mass of nearly two thousand persons congregated in the Hall field and when it was over the men committed were to be removed to Flint prison, and for greater safety it was resolved to send them to Flint by the way of Chester for the convenience of railway travelling. The mob was determined on a rescue; this feeling was anticipated by the magistrates, who, for the public security had obtained that day from Chester, a military escort of fifty men with their officers ; these were in addition to a guard of about forty of the regular Police force. About 7 p.m. the prisoners were escorted by this force, and accompanied by several magistrates to the Railway Station, but as soon as they emerged from the Hall field a continuous shower of stones was hurled at the Soldiers and Police, and the crowd pressed closer and closer on the guard ; the prisoners themselves making desperate efforts to escape ; by this time nearly half the guard, both Soldiers and Police were seriously wounded, the mob were so daring as to come to close quarters with the Soldiers, and try to get possession of their weapons ; all this time the guard made no other resistance than trying to push back the mob, and keep safe possession of their prisoners ; their Captain, Blake, was struck down seriously wounded, and many of the soldiers and police officers disabled, at length a magistrate gave the word to "fire,"—the result was, four deaths, one of them a young woman, innocent of the fray certainly— the other three, two men and one woman, evidently violent ringleaders, the woman was one of which there were too many among the mob, supplying the men with stones which they carried by laps full. The Riot Act was read, but not until most of the mischief was done. Of the Soldiers and Police, more than half their number were seriously hurt by the stones, one of the Military it was thought fatally so. The fifty Soldiers returned by train to their barracks at Chester that night, escorting the prisoners—whose release had been thus attempted—with their guard of Police thus far on their way to Flint Gaol,—but not until a fresh force of one hundred men had been telegraphed for, which arrived by returning train, who, with their officers, were amply furnished with shelter and accommodation in the rooms of the Market Hall.

At the inquest on the bodies a verdict of "justifiable homicide" was returned, and both Military and Police applauded for their long forbearance before retaliating on the mob.

A number of cavillers have objected that the Military were not justified in firing before the reading of the Riot Act, but they are amply discharged from all blame on that head by the public approbation of their conduct; but still more when the subject was referred to in the House of Commons, and the question asked of the Home Secretary if any fault could be attached to any of the authorities, he answered, the Military would, under the provocation they received, have been justified in using their weapons even earlier than they did, and without regarding whether the Riot Act had been read or not. Several of the rioters were subsequently arrested and tried at the ensuing Assizes held at Mold, August 6th, 1869, where, after a patient investigation lasting nearly three whole days, were found guilty by the jury. Five of them were sentenced each to Ten years penal servitude.

Since this affair, quiet has reigned in the town and neighbourhood, the rioting party apparently frightened at the effect of their outbreak.*

To proceed with our descriptions, the want of a Market Hall and Assembly Rooms, had long been felt a necessity in the town, the markets being held in the open street. The butchers had projecting sheds, called shambles, in front of some of the houses, others, moveable benches, and tables called standings, in the street; these were not only inconvenient but unwholsome, for in wet weather both buyer and seller were greatly inconvenienced, and in warm or dusty weather, the meat got soon spoiled; these objections the New Market Hall has entirely removed, and every one now wonders how the former state of things was permitted to exist so long as it did. A second Market House was built simultaneously with this Hall, and its stalls are chiefly occupied by butchers.

Even with this great accommodation the high street on full market days seems as liberally supplied with these moveable standings as before the market houses were built, this fact must be attributed to the great increase of trade carried on here of late years, a sufficient argument for their erection. The only per-

* A Lithographic Drawing of the Riot was published by Pring and Price.

ceptible difference is, no butcher's meat is now exposed for sale in the open street.

Upon a portion of the ground originally purchased for the County Hall purposes, new and capacious Militia Barracks have been erected; these contain accommodations for a permanent staff, and on the first floor of the building, is a very large armoury excellently well arranged and kept, and containing all necessary stores and accoutrements for supplying the companies of militia during their periodical trainings. The building was erected in 1858.

Near to these two buildings, and harmonising with them in the style of their architecture, stand the National Schools, built in 1849, and fitted with all appliances for instructing in separate apartments, each under their respective masters and mistresses, boys, girls, and infants, on an average numbering 350 children.

These three buildings group well together, and when viewed from a distance, form a most pleasing combination, and taken in connection with their surroundings, that is, the eastern end of the noble church, with its massive tower beyond, and the elegant vicarage house viewed in the background, which from the elevated nature of the ground are seen considerably above the tops of these public buildings, complete a most attractive and imposing picture.

There is also a British School, on an average numbering 200 children.

We will continue our perambulations about the town, and note its most prominent objects, and the first as most conspicuous is the Fountain and Clock at the Cross.

This erection had its origin in a meeting held at the County Hall in October, 1864, to do honour to the memory of the late Prince Albert, and through the spirited and unanimous temper of its promoters the result was this handsome memorial, combining as it does a central lamp post surmounted by a town clock, the lamps so arranged to throw their light on the face of the clock, that the time may be seen by night as well as day, while the base forms two drinking fountains surrounded by a flight of steps in the manner of market crosses in the olden time.

Bronze medallions each containing an excellent life-sized likeness of the late Prince Consort adorn two sides of the fountain, the legend around which tells, it is dedicated to the memory of "Albert the Good."

Near the Fountain is one of those useful erections, a pillar letter box, placed there in 1865. While on this spot we must not forget to look upon the new establishment, fitted up by the publishers of this work, Messrs. Pring and Price, replete as it is with every convenience necessary for carrying on a well-ordered printing, publishing and stationery concern, vieing in completeness with any business of the kind in the principality.

The next public building that will attract the visitor is the new Savings Bank, opened for public business in August 1869, an attractive and elegant building.

The Savings Bank in this town dates its establishment from March, 1818. Having been held in the same room from its first opening, and its profits during these years amounting to over £1,000, it was deemed fitting that its jubilee should be celebrated by making for it a new home. The Trustees of the establishment after certifying that all demands of its numerous depositors were secured, determined to build a new bank with its surplus funds, and being fortunate in securing an admirable site, the present erection is the result.

The public buildings next in importance are the places of worship. First is the Calvinistic Chapel, an elegant erection in New-street, with a beautiful and massive Corinthian Portico. Next a new Chapel for the English Wesleyan Methodists, a red brick erection, opened in 1869. The Welsh Wesleyan body has a commodious chapel conspicuously and well situated at the higher part of the main street; indeed most of the branches of the great dissenting bodies have chapels in the town, as the Welsh Independents and the Baptists. The Roman Catholics also have their Chapel and School-house near the town.

Of the elegant Parish Church, a full description of its interior is given in the Rambles, its exterior is equally elegant as may be perceived by the view attached as a frontispiece to this work, it likewise enjoys the advantage of a good situation, being built on a commanding eminence overlooking the houses in the town, the ascertained date of its erection is 1500, but a still older religious building occupied the ground ere this was erected.

On a high bank overlooking the Railway Station stands the neat Church belonging to the Nonconformist body termed the Free Church, the first stone of which was laid 5th November, 1863. This is a commodious Gothic erection and amply fulfils the mission for which it was promoted.

And now that we have reached the Railway Station let us pause awhile and reflect on the mighty means that has mainly contributed to develop the resources of this town thereby bringing it up to its present state of prosperity.

That great work the London and Holyhead Railway, necessarily required branches or feeders to sustain it, and one of the most important was the small arm from Chester to Mold. Originally formed for the purpose of uniting a rich mineral district with England, it has had the effect of opening one of the prettiest vallies in Great Britain, that, through which the river Alun flows down to the river Dee. The whole of this valley is fertile and beautiful, and now that the line is opened from Wrexham to Mold, the valley is accessible from the grand old castle at Caergwrle to the lofty mound at Mold, on which the Castle of Mont Alto formerly stood. Extended as it was this past summer, so as to join the Vale of Clwyd Railway at Denbigh, the line passes through one of those beautiful mountain limestone districts which are rare in Great Britain though not in Ireland. Except for the want of lakes it is scarcely possible to conceive a more lovely scene than that which is presented from the top of the mound at Mold. This charming district is completely thrown open by the extension of the line from Mold into the Vale of Clwyd. Another branch,—viz., from Mold to Wrexham, through Nerquis and the great coal district is in progress, and will be completed as speedily as possible.

The extension of the Mold line unites it with the Vale of Clwyd Railway between Denbigh and St. Asaph. This line was constructed chiefly to throw open one of the most beautiful vales in Europe, and it will be opened more completely by its connection with the Mold line.

Apart from the Mineral and Agricultural products of Mold and its neighbourhood, which constituted the trade of the town, at the latter end of the past century, and when the cotton trade of the kingdom had partially developed the greatness it ultimately arrived at, a noble spinning Factory was erected near the town. It may be asked, why was so large an establishment erected in such an out-of-the-way place as Mold? The reply is, a plentiful and even supply of water was at all times to be found here, and moreover labour for the mill could be had at a very much lower charge than in the great manufacturing towns; although the expense of carriage of the raw and manufactured material was great, still the concern was worked at a profit. It employed about 250 persons working about 25,000 spindles; but on Thursday, 8th November, 1866, the inhabitants of the town were astonished at their morning meal with the alarming news that the "Cotton Mill," as it was termed, had been entirely destroyed by fire in the night, and for so great a conflagration, the wonder was, that it could have occurred without an alarm being heard in the town, although it stood at their very doors; no enquiries set on foot could ascertain how the fire originated, and up to the present time it remains a mystery.

The property destroyed was insured for £26,000, but that sum fell far short of its real worth, and the loss happening at a time when the cotton market was in a very depressed condition, there was no inducement to build it up again, and to this day its ruins remain nearly in the same state as when the fire had done its worst, and the poor families that were almost ruined by it, have, most of them, sought other homes to labour in for their subsistence.

Next in importance, though it ought to have stood first, we must notice the mineral products of the place.

Flintshire, as is well known, is a great mineral county,—Lead, Coal, Ironstone, Limestone, Fire clay ; &c., being found in abundance throughout. The Lead Mines, though not very productive at present, have in past times, afforded great quantities; there is little doubt but that the lead mines at Maes-y-safn were known to and worked by the Romans during their occupation of the island; and to this day, the mines at this place are the most productive in the neighbourhood, and well worth a visit of inspection. A water wheel of 52 feet diameter being a most picturesque object when seen working its long rows of rods pumping water from a great depth in the mine.

The coal products of the county would afford material for quite a history in themselves. Traditionary and indeed documentary evidence exists to prove, that coal has been raised in Flintshire from a very remote period, dating from the reign of Edward the First; still from the methods of procuring it, it might be called but a mere scratching of the surface, and up to the present time, even with all the mechanical appliances used in its getting, geologists affirm that, greater quantities, in much thicker seams, underlies all that has hitherto been worked.

Mr. Hall, a gentleman attached to the Government Geological Survey, has stated there scarcely remains a reasonable doubt of the continuation of the coal formation from Flintshire to Lancashire, under the beds of the Dee and Mersey.

A wonderful impetus was given to the coal trade by the discovery of beds of cannel coal at Leeswood, just at the time when the oil fever of America was startling the world. Oil works in great abundance, and some of equally great extent sprung up in our neighbourhood as if by magic, and speculation rose in a very little time to fever heat, but almost as suddenly collapsed ; the market got overstocked, and has never recovered its buoyancy, most of these great oil works have stopped working, and their plant and materials gone to the hammer, but a few still continue to struggle on.

Rich as the bowels of the earth in Flintshire are in mineral wealth, its surface is nevertheless as productive as many purely agricultural districts, and in no part of the County is it seriously disfigured by the effects of the underground workings. It can still supply all its inhabitants with farm produce and has large herds of cattle and flocks of sheep to send away periodically to the English markets, and much corn to spare also.

Among the products of the locality are Fire-brick Clay, Common-brick Clay, and Pottery Clay of every description, the latter sort of Clay being worked into all manner of forms of which it is susceptible, at Buckley, near Mold ; the working of Clay in this place is its specialty, and the people themselves are a very special people, speaking a dialect, that seems a mixture of the English and Welsh languages and the broadest of the Staffordshire, Lancashire, and Shropshire dialects, indeed it is not an uncommon thing to hear some of the people of the place boast of being able to speak three languages, viz:—English, Welsh, and Buckley.

It may be important to inform Tourists and Strangers, that Mold contains all that could be wished for, in point of accommodation, having excellent Hotels and Inns. In the front rank stands the Black Lion Hotel, a first class establishment, with every accommodation required, from a house of its character; next in place are the Royal Oak; the Star; the Dolphin; and Victoria Hotels; the King's Head; the Red Lion; and the Boar's Head Inns, equally good in point of conveniences and comforts, the managers of each of these establishments, with their aids considering it a chief duty, to make their customers feel they are at home. Besides the above named, Mold has a great number of minor houses of refreshment.

The banks are, the National Provincial Bank of England, and the North and South Wales Bank.

The Shops are numerous and extensive and of the kinds usually met with in Towns in England, all well supplied with goods, and with the Railway accommodation, having its electric telegraph establishment connected with it, there are few human wants not to be found in the town, but can be had at a short notice.

The Gentlemen's seats around the town are many, all picturesquely situated, a few may be named—as Leeswood, the seat of John Wynne Eyton, Esq., Tower; Nerquis Hall; Pentrehobin; Leeswood Hall; Hartsheath Park; Plas Teg; Plas Issa; Soughton Hall; Llwyn Offa; Llwynegryn; Rhual; Gwysaney; Coed-Du; Penbedw; Colomendy; Glanrafon; Fron Hall; Hafod; Bryn Coch; Preswylfa; Maesyffynnon, &c.— Of late years, since the Vale has become more known to the public, numerous parties from a distance

Moel Famma.

Moel Famma is about 1850 ft. above the level of the sea. The Monument is in the Egyptain style, about 150 ft. high and 60 ft. in diameter at the base.

visit it to enjoy its beauties. A very favorite journey of tourists from here, is to the mountain called Moel Famma, seven miles from this town to its summit, on the highest part of this mountain, was erected, in the year 1811, a lofty monument, to commemorate the anniversary of the fiftieth year of the reign of George third; this year called the jubilee year was remarkable for being kept with great rejoicings all over the kingdom; the government of the day took the lead, but the call was eagerly and unanimously responded to by the municipalities of the kingdom, and by other public bodies, and societies; and the great mass of the population hailed the 25th of October, 1810, with every demonstration of loyalty, attachment, and respect. It was truly a national spectacle, and a gay and beautiful one. The jubilee was observed as a holiday, in every city, town, village, and hamlet in the kingdom. A singular coincidence which rendered this jubilee the more remarkable, was, that the three monarchs of Britain, whose reign extended beyond half a century were those, each the third of his respective name,— viz:—Henry third, fifty-six years; Edward third, fifty-one years; and George third, sixty years.

The inhabitants of Flintshire and Denbighshire amply proved their loyalty on the occasion, by subscribing to erect this conspicuous and costly building, and the choice of situation was a most happy one, since from this spot is viewed a scene, matchless in the whole island, namely,—the entire range of the Vale of Clwyd, in its length and breadth, and embracing in the distant view, the mountains of Snowdon to the right, and Aran, and Cader Idris, to the left. The monument itself is a very conspicuous object from long distances on land, and is also seen as a land-mark from many miles off, far out at sea.

A sad calamity however visited it in the year 1864, in a storm of unusual severity in that year, the upper half, or pyramidal portion of it, was blown down, but fortunately, the falling stones did not do irreparable injury to the lower part, which still presents its massive form to the view of the world at large; but it is to be regretted, that the ruins remain as the storm left them, and no effort has been made to restore it to its former state, even in the useful capacity of a public land-mark.

Another favorite excursion from here is to Halkin Mountain, four miles distance, to ascend the hill, popularly known as Moel-y-Gaer, but more correctly, Moel-y-Crio; Moel-y-Gaer being a name common to several of these British Posts, at least there are three in this neighbourhood called Moel-y-Gaer, there may be others known by that title in the long line of these ancient defences.

This elevation on Halkin Mountain, is remarkable as one of these British Posts in an almost perfect state, being nearly a complete circle, of a deep ditch, and a high bank, formed of earth and loose stones, with its two entrances. These Posts are of very great antiquity, they must have been used merely as shelters, for the women and children, and flocks, and herds, of the inhabitants of the country, during the time of any sudden invasion; for they are generally found to be destitute of water, which is evidence they could not have been intended for places of long abode; they are always placed within sight of each other, so that by the common signal of fire, notice could be given of the approach of an enemy.

A long list could be compiled of them as reaching from Dyserth near Rhyl, right across the country to the mouth of the Severn.

The hill called Moel-y-Crio, appears to be partly artificial; an enormous undertaking to pile up so vast a body of earth; but it was necessary at this spot, as it is the continuous Post between Moel-y-Gaer, in Northop Parish, and the Post called Moel Arthur, near Nannerch.

An idea of the vastness of these Posts may be had, when it is remembered, that the one next Moel Arthur, in the line of defence, on Bryn-y-Cloddiau, or the hill of ditches, is a mile and a half in circuit, defended by single, double, triple, and even quadruple ditches.

To return to Mold, little more remains to be said. Of its picturesqueness and beauty, stranger tourists, visiting the place, generally express their admiration. Of its changes, there is one extensive alteration yet to be mentioned. Mold has always been the Assize Town of the County, but the County Gaol is situated at Flint, six miles distant; this has been long felt an inconvenience, and of late years more prison accommodation being required it was deemed better by the authorities, to build a New Gaol, than add to the old one, the consequence is, a new, commodious, and most extensive building, with every needful requirement for such an establishment, has been erected within half a mile's distance from Mold, and before the close of this year, viz :—1869, it is expected it will be in full use, whether to the benefit of the population of Mold Parish, containing 10,500 and the County at large remains to be seen.

In taking a review of the changes and alterations in the Town of Mold, with its population of 4,000, it is obvious that all the important additions have been made to it during the past thirty years; the great lever has been the Railway, for without it, the resources of Mold, might have lain dormant for another long period.

In thus reviewing any period within our own experience, every one of us is apt to exaggerate the gains of the time,—that is its gains, as contrasted with what we know or read of what was the state of society, say in a period of thirty or forty years before. This arises in part from confounding change or expansion in our own ideas, with change in the world about us. It may be hoped we may look without pride or vanity upon such improvements as can be recognised, while their review will be thoroughly delightful as convincing us of that partial advance which we humbly but firmly trust to be the destination of the human race.

Before concluding this paper, it may be necessary to ask for the charitable construction of the reader, that he should not think that much which is here noted, is of too trivial and simple a nature to be recorded in the form of a book; but let him imagine how interesting it would be now, if we could get it,—the record of all the trivialities of Mold, a hundred years ago; this sounds somewhat arrogant we must confess, assuming, as it does, that the present work is to be interesting a century hence; but the remark is not intended to convey that idea, the author, in compiling these notices, endeavoured to employ his leisure hours, and if he aspires to any character in the work, it is that of being thought

" A snapper up of unconsidered trifles."

List of Subscribers to the 2000 Edition

W.E. & S. Ackers	Halkyn
Michael Adams	Hawarden
Alun School	Mold
Wendy Anderton	Mold
Patricia Andrews-Roberts	Mold
Colin E. Antwis	Mynydd Isa
John & Ann Atkinson	Mold
Mr. Ray Bailey	Saltney
Norman & Valerie Barker	Ewloe
Elizabeth Bartlett	Leeswood
Peter Baston	Buckley
Monica Bayliss	Caergwrle
Dave Beck	Wallasey
David Bell	Calstock, Cornwall
Ann Bent	Mold
Grenville Bevan	Mold
Mrs Gwyneth Bill	Nannerch
Cllr. R. C. Bithell	Chairman of Education and Recreation Committee
Mr. Roger Bletcher	Mold
Christine Bloomfield	Flint
Edward G. Booker	Northop
Joan Bradley	Mold
G. R. Briggs	Chester
Alun Broughton	Rhosesmor
Colin and Margaret Brown	Buckley
Glenys Bruce	Rhydymwyn
W. G. Bryan	Mold
Bryn Coch Primary School	Mold
Mrs M. A. Cafearo	Buckley
D. Cassell	Abermorddu
Alice Clack	Mold

E. & S.M. Cocker	Gwernymynydd
Jill Collins	Mold
Lesley E. Courtney	Mynydd Isa
Hazel Coyle	Mynydd Isa
Jim Daley	Mold
John and Elinor Davidson	Halkyn
David M. Davies	Yr Wyddgrug
Elizabeth Ann Davies	Gwernymynydd
E. Roger LL. Davies	Gwernymynydd
Joanne Clare Davies	Buckley
R. & Y. P. Davies	Penyffordd
Ray Davies	Mold
Richard Davies	Rhyl
R. D. Davies	Mold
P. G. Dear	Bryn y Baal
Paul Dendy	Treuddyn
Derwen Primary School	Higher Kinnerton
Michael Devlin	Mynydd Isa
Mr. Norman Eastwood	Gwernymynydd
Ann Edwards	Nercwys
Hywel Wyn Edwards	Sychdyn
Joan Edwards	Buckley
John Wyn Edwards	Holywell
Bryn Ellis	Halkyn
High J. Ellis	Mold
Dr. Morton E. Evans	Denbigh
Dr. R. Paul Evans	Wrexham
Gaynor Faircloth	Mold
Paul Faircloth	Mold
Mrs Joan Farmer	Mold
John Foden	Broughton
Barbara Forbes	Buckley
Hazel A. Formby	Ysceifiog
John Foulkes	Mold
Mervyn Foulkes	Padeswood

Peggy Grace	Gwernymynydd
Mr. & Mrs D. Griffith	Minera
D. L. Griffiths	Mold
Miss Rhiannon E. Griffiths	Mold
M. Haffenden	Higher Kinnerton
Joy Nicola Haime	Mold
M. E. Hanrahan	Ewloe
Clifford Harley	Mold
H. V. Harley	Mold
Trevor Harley	Mold
Vera N. Harley	Birmingham
R. D. Harold	Mold
F. Raymond Harris	Mold
Lin Hawtin	Llanferres
J. G. Hill	Mancot
Mrs Mary Hill	Buckley
Mr. & Mrs T. E. Hipkiss	Penyffordd
Holywell High School	Holywell
Ewart L. Hughes	Bersham
G. A. Hughes	Llong
N. A. Hughes	Mold
Kim & Ray Humphreys	Northop
John Summers High School	Queensferry
D. T. R. & S. Johnson	Hawarden
Carol Jones	Pantymwyn
C. A. Jones	Sychdyn
Dafydd Meirion Jones	Yr Wyddgrug
Dr. Timothy LL. Jones	Gwernaffield
Glyn & Winifred Jones	Hawarden
Graham & Lilian Jones	Buckley
J. Howard Jones	Buckley
Mr. & Mrs Dennis Jones	Mold
Mr. & Mrs Gareth D. Jones	Buckley
Mr. William A. Jones	Rhydymwyn
Mr. W. Nigel Jones	Mold

Nia Wyn Jones	Bwcle
Pamela Jones	Mold
Cllr. T. W. Jones OBE	Chairman of Flintshir
Terry Kavanagh	Hawarden
John Kay	Mold
Brenda Kelly	Mold
Tony King	Maeshafn
Patricia Laing	Mold
Mr. P. Latham	Minera
Jim Law	Mold
J. G. Ledsham	Mold
Leeswood Community Council	Leeswood
David Lewis	Mold
Gordon A. Limb	Llong
Vicente Llinares	Mold
A. Wyn Lloyd	Llanfair D. C.
Llyfrgell Genedlaethol Cymru	Aberystwyth
Krissi Lobely	Wirral
B. A. Lowens	Nercwys
Paul F. Mason	Gwernymynydd
John Stuart Mather	Gwernymynydd
Alison Matthews	Penyffordd
Chris McDade	Mold
H. G. Mclean	Prestatyn
Irene Morgans	Sychdyn
David J. Morris	Northop Hall
G. E. Morris	Pantymwyn
Ian Munro	Penyffordd
Keith Mutch	Mold
D. J. F. Nancarrow	Mynydd Isa
Joan Neal	Mold
Rosemary E. Nicholls	Nercwys
Bruce W. Noble	Holywell
Jean and Frederick O'Brien	Mold
Peter Orton	Pontybodkin

A. X. & E. Owens	Hawarden
Christopher Paul Owens	Bagillt
David M. Owens	New Brighton
Doreen Parker	Rhostyllen
Mr. & Mrs J. K. Parker	Rhyl
Ann Parry	Mold
Edward C. Parry-Jones	Trelogan
Katherine Peglar	Cilcain
W. O. Piercy Esq.	Nercwys
Marie Pipkin	Gwernaffield
Andy Polakowski	Mold
Raymond & Rena Powell	Mold
Richard & Meira Powell	Mold
Bethany Grace Price	Oldham
Mrs S. Price	Sychdyn
Molly May Price	Oldham
The Venerable T. W. Pritchard	Hawarden
Mr. Ernest Probert	Mold
Bronwen & Gordon Ramsay	Northop
Lawrence Rawsthorne	Sychdyn
Mrs I. M. Read	Mold
Marjorie Gore Rees	Gwernaffield
P. John Richards	Halkyn
Olwen Richardson	Mold
William Rimmer	Buckley
Alison Laurie Roberts	Mold
David F. Roberts	Nannerch
Eifion Roberts	Buckley
Elwyn & Mona Roberts	Rhuthun
Gail Roberts	Penyffordd
Gladys L. Roberts	Buckley
James John Roberts	Mynydd Isa
Pedr Roberts	Mold
Ray & Ingrid Roberts	Mynydd Isa
Richard Wyn Roberts	Mold

V. & J. D. Roberts	Broughton
Wynne Roberts	Gwernaffield
Robert Robins	Wirral
Brian G. Robinson	Mold
Janet Robinson	Llandegla
D. S. & G. M. Rogers	Mold
D. Rowe	Mold
W. R. & B. C. Rowley	Mold
Sandycroft C. P. School	Mancot
R. J. Shannon	Mold
R. A. B. Sheffield	Mold
Audrey Sinnott	Broughton
David Smart	Mynydd Isa
Howard Smith	Mold
R. G. Smith	Sychdyn
John & Stephen Speed	Mold
Gordon Stanley	Chester
M. A. Statham	Ewloe
Katie & Jim Steele	Mynydd Isa
Mr. Roger Sykes	Sychdyn
Mr. & Mrs F. E. Tanton	Minera
C. A. and A. Taylor	Penyffordd
Michael P. Taylor	New Brighton
Peter A. Taylor	Mynydd Isa
John Thomas	Rhoesesmor
Mrs Kate Thomas	Sychdyn
M. Thompson	Ewloe Green
V. Thomson	Mold
Helen Tomlinson	Mold
P. W. Trinder	Hawarden
Mrs Barbara Turnbull	Connah's Quay
Mrs Christina Tyndall	Bryn y Baal
Jen Walker	New Brighton
Mrs S. Walls	Halkyn
John & Enid Walters	Sychdyn

Joseph Wareing	Buckley
Jean Webb	Pantymwyn
Derek & Lyn Western	Wem
F. White	Mynydd Isa
Howard White	Mold
Barry Williams	Sholing, Southampton
Beryl Drury Williams	Mold
Delyth Williams	Cilcain
Elizabeth Jean Williams	Mold
Glyn Williams	Brynford
Kevin Williams	Mold
Mr. K. H. Williams	Mold
Philip Drury Williams	Mold
Ron & Olwen Williams	Holywell
Verity Williams	Hope Mountain
Vida Williams	Mold
Annie (Nancy) Wilson	Mold
Meirlys and David Witton-Davies	Mold
Michael Wright	Mold
Ysgol Bro Carmel	Holywell

This book is no.

053

**of a limited edition
of 500 copies**